Mike Sullivan's l  f
international show
guided the fortun
stars in the world

'There's No People Like Show People' is Sullivan's story
of his friends and enemies among the best-known names
in the world.

In it he tells how he discovered SHIRLEY BASSEY,
groomed her for stardom – and then lost her. 'I turned
her into the biggest, hottest property in the business,' he
says 'and in doing it I created a nightmare for myself.'

He guided DICK EMERY through his marriages and
romances, saved him from a blackmailing pimp, and tells
how they were once inseparable.

For the first time Mike Sullivan tells the true stories
behind the public face of SID JAMES, one of Britain's
best-loved comics. Sullivan promoted Sid to star status...
and star money. But he couldn't stop him gambling away
a fortune. He protected him from 'heavies' who came to
collect Sid's gambling debts... and was himself 'conned'
by his client!

James, says Sullivan 'had a face like an unmade bed', but
he saw himself as a great lover and this book reveals the
secret romance between Sid and 'Carry On' star
BARBARA WINDSOR.

Among the other top names in Sullivan's story are:

MARILYN MONROE: When the Hollywood sex
goddess was involved in a love triangle, Mike Sullivan was
called in to help... and was banned from a major studio
as a result.'

ROGER MOORE: Sullivan gave the screen's James Bond his first job in show business and '007' Moore later repaid him by saving him from a deadly spider.

ERROL FLYNN: From 'cat houses' in Tijuana through a 200 mile pub crawl in Britain, an hilarious encounter with a colonial governor and a fight in a Paris hotel, Sullivan drank and brawled around the world with Flynn.

AVA GARDNER: She came to dinner at Sullivan's English country home – with embarrassing results!

These are but a few of the major stars who have figured in his life. Others include BING CROSBY, DICK HAYMES, PETER SELLERS, NORMAN WISDOM, HARRY SECOMBE, FRANK SINATRA, SHANI WALLIS and DANY ROBIN, the glamorous French film star who he wooed and later married after breaking up one of the most enduring and popular marriages in Europe.

Mike Sullivan was also responsible for the making of 'Goal!', the story of the 1966 World Cup and the most successful football movie ever made.

And when he took it on he was broke and had never seen a football match!

In 'There's No People Like Show People', Mike Sullivan conceals nothing. 'I have nothing to be ashamed of and nothing to hide', he says.

There has never been a franker, more revealing story of the stars, their shimmering life-styles and their tarnished secrets.

There's No People Like
SHOW PEOPLE

Confessions of a Showbiz Agent

By Michael Sullivan

QUADRANT BOOKS

THERE'S NO PEOPLE LIKE SHOW PEOPLE

Copyright © 1982 Michael Sullivan and Tom Merrin

First published in Great Britain in 1984 by
Quadrant Books Limited, Newcombe House, Notting Hill Gate,
London W11 3LQ.

All rights reserved. No part of this publication may be
reproduced or transmitted, in any form or by any means, without
permission of the publishers.

Typset by Avocet
Printed by William Collins Sons & Co Ltd.

ISBN 0 946894-05-1

Photographs courtesy Daily Mirror, London,
first section page 7 and top page 8.
Second section top right page 2, page 3
top page 4, page 5 and top page 8. Third
section page 1. Courtesy Camera Press
Ltd, London, third section top page 2.
Courtesy P A Reuter Photos, London, third
section bottom page 2. Courtesy BBC
London, first section bottom page 8.
Courtesy National Film Archives, London,
second section bottom page 4.

'All the world's a stage, and I've had one hell of a life upon it.'

SULLIVAN AND SHAKESPEARE
(Who needs second billing!)

This book is dedicated to all my fellow agents who spend ninety per cent of their energy in the interests of artistes and are rewarded with only ten per cent of their earnings!

Contents

Overture   1

And Beginners   3

Act One
Scene One   : Sid James   12
Scene Two   : Errol Flynn   27
Scene Three   : A Brush with the Stars   38
Scene Four   : The Stars and Their Lovers   55
Scene Five   : Publicity Stunts   72

Act Two
Scene One   : Dick Emery   85
Scene Two   : 'Carry on Trying'   95
Scene Three   : The Funny Men   97
Scene Four   : The Power Men   109

Act Three
Scene One   : The Girl from Tiger Bay   118
Scene Two   : Shirley's Ascending Star   138
Scene Three   : International Stardom   156
Scene Four   : Press Revelations   182
Scene Five   : Shirley Bassey's Marriage   201

Act Four
Scene One   : My Five Wives   213

False Tabs   225

List of illustrations

My father, Sir Frederick Allen
My mother, Rosa
Sir Arthur Sullivan
Sisters Three
A proud keepsake
At the age of 6
In 1939
My sister Sheila
Sid James
Jack Douglas
Carry on London
Errol Flynn
Dick Haymes and Family
Roger Moore
Michael Parkinson

} Between pages 36 and 37

Sean Connery and golfing friends
Eric Sykes
Bing Crosby
Dean Martin
Kirk Douglas and family
Marilyn Monroe
Bruce Forsyth
Ava Gardner
Kathy Kirby
Humphrey Bogart
Shani Wallis
Shani Wallis Stunt
The Waltz of the Torridors
Dick Emery
Jimmy Tarbuck

} Between pages 108 and 109

List of illustrations – continued

Shirley Bassey
Shirley Bassey and first husband
Jack Hylton and wife
Ex-wives, Juhni, Kitten and Lily
Alfred Hitchcock
George Sanders
Wedding to Dany Robin
Ted Rogers
Des O'Connor
Wedding Ball
Dany and grandchildren
At home in Marbella
Now and Forever

Between pages 180 and 181

OVERTURE...

Sometimes I feel sorry for agents. The feeling doesn't last long. I can usually find something about them to rapidly change my mood. But in my brief moments of sympathy I try to remember all the things they are required to be when dealing with a star. It's a formidable list: friend, confidante, sex therapist, doctor, psychiatrist, soothsayer, fashion designer, booking clerk, public relations expert, minder, chauffeur, drinking companion, secretary, fender-off of bores and eternal provider of witty conversation. In short, more often than not, the star demands that the agent be everything from a Knight in Shining Armour to a Fool with a Cap of Bells. All this, and he is required to count the money at the same time.

Not many survive the course. Those that do are a remarkable breed of men, an elite band of survivors who have come through the toughest assault course in showbiz. Michael Sullivan is one such. There is not much of him but what there is could be melted down and used to tip an armour piercing rocket. I first met him many years ago in Spain when over long and happy dinners we engaged in conversations that now, I realise, form the chapters of this book. It's a fascinating account of the kid from nowhere who made a name both for himself and many of the people he represented. The book is very much like the man himself; cheeky, irreverent, opinionated, flamboyant, erratic... but never, never boring.

Michael Parkinson

AND BEGINNERS

In the days when there were two hundred and forty pennies to the English pound and the coin itself still had some purchasing power there was, next to the old Alhambra Theatre in London's Leicester Square, a pin-table saloon with a shooting gallery at the far end.

It was a short walk from Regent Street where I worked as a 15 year old office boy in Tom Pacey's theatrical agency and on the sort of money I was earning I had to take my pleasures where I could find them... and for as cheaply as I could.

If getting a little fun could also be turned into a profit, however small, that was a welcome bonus and I found the answer to both in that gaudy catch-penny arcade. I became so adept at winning five cigarettes for a penny during my lunch hours that one day the proprietor of the place stopped me.

'Son, I'll give you two hundred cigarettes as a once and for all-time payment if you stay out of here,' he said.

I took the deal, but I did not stay out of the place, although I stopped playing the machines and would hang around talking to the man who ran it.

We became friendly and one week-end he took me to Southend-on-Sea, the town on the North side of the River Thames estuary that was the East London Cockneys' 'Coney Island'. At the Kursaal, the great amusement park just off the sea front, my new friend owned a number of side shows. As we toured the place he showed me his shooting range and darts stalls and other attractions in which he had an interest.

But the thing that grabbed my interest was his freak show: 'The Only Five-Legged Sheep In Captivity'.

I stood spellbound as the barker went into his 'spiel' for the crowds and then pushed my luck by telling the boss that I thought I could do better.

'If you can, you can start next week-end', was the answer — and I did.

For drawing in the crowds on summer Saturdays and Sundays I was paid one pound a day, a third as much again as I earned at my regular job. I had the time of my life, shouting lies, wearing a straw hat and carrying a cane, and what I learned with that freak show formed my philosophy of show business.

Lashed by my glib tongue, people paid sixpence each to see the five-legged sheep. They trooped inside the tent and walked around a roped-off circle. Inside that circle was a stuffed sheep with an obviously phoney extra leg stuck to its flank!

A large printed notice at the back of the tent announced: 'You have been fooled, but don't tell your friends'.

What that five-legged sheep taught me was this: We were fooling the people but they still laughed and went away not telling their friends because they did not want to admit they had been taken in.

But what if we were NOT fooling them? What if there was an attraction inside that lived up to my bragging?

Then they would not walk away silently. They would be urging their friends to see it and there could be four hundred, not forty, standing in line to pay their money.

I made up my mind that when I became a showman in my own right I would always have an attraction that could be flamboyantly advertised; that it would live up to the 'spiel' and what people got for their money must be something they could go away and talk about.

The fifth leg on that tattered stuffed sheep was a classic piece of show business hokum.

In this story some of the 'sheep' are so much larger than life that they have many more than five legs. The difference is that it's not hokum and I want you to tell your friends about it...

From the moment of my birth I was ideally suited in at least one particular to become a theatrical agent:

I am a bastard.

In the world of entertainment it is a word so frequently levelled against the members of my calling that 'agent' is rarely uttered without its accompaniment.

This is because most of the time the people who deal with agents and for whom they in turn deal regard them as little more than a necessary evil and have to cushion their grief at having to part with ten per cent of their earnings (which would only go to the tax man if they didn't) by resorting to abuse.

Their vilification of a hard-working professional is, in the main, totally unjustified. In my own case I could always console myself with the thought that maybe the client (for once accurate) was merely referring to an accident of birth rather than my integrity.

Well, that's my excuse...

Even my bastardy was different from others. The circumstances of my birth are so bizarre that they are worth recording in detail. Where else would you encounter a half-brother and half-sister who are also natural cousins?

In the latter part of the nineteenth century the greatest principal boy in that peculiarly English theatrical institution the pantomime was Kate Sullivan. She was a niece of Sir Arthur Sullivan of Gilbert and Sullivan operetta fame and the fact that Kate and her uncle hated each other's guts did not seem to have the slightest effect, beneficial or adverse, on her professional success.

Katie in time gave birth to three daughters: Kate Jnr, Josephine and Rosa. They were all beautiful and all followed their mother into the theatre.

In 1916 Josephine Sullivan met and fell in love with a dapper, handsome man in the shipping business called Frederick Allen. Later he was destined for a knighthood and the managing directorship of the huge P and O shipping concern. In the early days of their romance he was establishing himself in the commercial world... and already married. He was also the chairman of the Port of London Authority and his successful intervention in dockland industrial disputes earned him the nickname 'The Peacemaker'.

For the sake of the propriety which existed in those days when millions of young men were being sent to their deaths in the obscenity of the First World War, their love affair was kept a close secret. But it became an embarrassing confidence when, early in 1917 Josephine became pregnant.

In the September of that year she died giving birth to a daughter Sheila. In a way her death may have taken some of the pressures of the clandestine affair off Frederick Allen. There was now no chance that he could be called upon to marry Josephine and any attempts to prove parentage would be difficult ... even if such a course were taken, which it was not.

Sheila was handed over to her mother's sister Kate, a musical comedy star who had retired when her husband died after being gassed in the trenches.

Kit, as she was called by the family, became Sheila's 'illegitimate' mother and Frederick Allen continually tried to make amends for the tragedy of his love affair with offers to support both Kit and the little girl, but these were generally refused.

Then, two or three years after Sheila's birth, Frederick Allen was caught up in one of the incredible twists of fate that occur more often in novels than real life. He fell in love again. This time with Josephine's sister Rosa.

Their affair was as secretive as that between the fast-rising shipping man and Josephine Sullivan had been, and it followed the same pattern in that, in 1921, Rosa Sullivan became pregnant and on October 23 of that year she gave birth to a boy, Michael, in a London nursing home.

That boy was me.

Like my half-sister and first cousin Sheila, I was given into the care of aunt Kit and lived with her believing that she was my real mother and Sheila my real sister. This conviction was shared by Sheila.

Kit, Sheila and I lived in Balham in South London where we were frequently visited by Rosa Sullivan – known to us as Auntie 'Woe' – a pet name born of Rosa's inability as a small child to pronounce her own correctly.

On two of those visits to our house Rosa was accompanied by an elegant, well-dressed man. He treated Sheila and myself kindly but any show of affection was reserved and hardly noticeable. Sir Frederick Allen, by now knighted and a major power in the shipping world, played his part in keeping the family secret. I thought he was my uncle.

My tight little world collapsed in the summer of 1934. I was 12 years old and had left home early one morning to go to a local swimming pool. On the way back, for a 'dare', I tried to race a bus. I was knocked down and rushed to hospital with severe injuries, particularly to my left leg which was saved from amputation by the skill of an Australian doctor called Williamson.

However, my injuries were so bad that I spent more than six months in that hospital and in the September – a month before my thirteenth birthday – the accident was followed by an even more traumatic event.

Sir Frederick Allen died and in the house in Balham on a Sunday afternoon over tea Kit and Rosa decided that I should be told the truth of my parentage.

Sheila already knew and had done so for two years. She had been sitting her matriculation examination and had to complete forms which called for details of her mother and father. She learned the truth and the shock of it has never really left her.

With remarkable psychological insight Rosa and Kit elected Sheila as the one to go to the hospital and tell me the story of my birth.

Sheila and I were very close to each other and she sat by my hospital bed and broke the news as gently as she could. She was terrified of the effect it might have upon me. I listened to her story and at the end of it I felt confused and disturbed. But as I reflected upon it I thought I had been given the greatest heritage I could wish for... a father, not even in name only, but a father who had been a man of substance, wealth and success. Somebody I could admire and want to copy.

Eventually I left hospital and returned to my education. Formal academic experience has never figured large in my life. This can probably be attributed to the fact that when I was four my aunt Kit was politely asked to remove me from a convent school at Balham and two years later my teachers at Clapham College, a day school run by Xavierian brothers, recommended that I might do better if I went instead to another Xavierian college at Mayfield in Sussex as a boarder.

I enjoyed life at Mayfield. They had a code that you were not guilty of anything unless you were actually caught doing it. I learned not to be caught and I have stuck rigidly to this code throughout my life.

After leaving hospital I was told that there was no longer enough money in the family for me to continue at Mayfield (maybe my father had been more frequent and generous with his support than I believed) and I was sent to Clark's College, a commercial school where I would learn shorthand and typing.

The shorthand didn't stick, but the typing did and at fourteen I left Clark's to apply for a job as an office boy to a cigar importer named Schishka in Imperial House, Regent Street, in London's West End.

This was in 1936. Jobs were scarce and when I arrived at the office on a Saturday morning I was seventh in line of a group of boys of my own age. Twenty minutes later we had not moved and I realised that the interviews had not started. I asked the next boy in the line for the Gents. He pointed the way and I wandered off.

I used the trip to the lavatory to find my way around the offices and on the way back I dropped in on the boss and talked myself into a job at one pound ten shillings for a seven day week. I scurried furtively past the line of waiting boys as I left.

I soon grew bored with working for Schishka. He was out of the office most of the time, leaving me to answer the telephone and type an average of three letters a day. I filled in time by practising copy typing.

The board by the door of Imperial House listed three theatrical agencies among the tenants. With my family background, show business was a natural calling for me and I told the lift boy at the building: 'If you ever hear of one of these agencies wanting an office boy, tell me. I'll give you my first week's wages if I get the job.'

Two weeks later the lift boy came running. 'The boy in Tom Pacey's office was fired last night.'

It was eleven o'clock on a Saturday morning. I had been working for Schishka for just six weeks. I left the office, walked to the door of the Pacey agency, knocked and walked in.

A man with a long cigar was sitting at a desk. He asked: 'What do you want?'

'I've come about the vacancy for an office boy.'

He looked surprised.

'How do you know there's a vacancy?'

'I understand your office boy has left.' I felt that to say 'fired' would be tactically wrong.

'Come in and sit down,' said the man whose name was Jack Sullivan. We tried to trace a relationship, but there was none. Anyway, sharing the same surname may have helped. Sullivan, who was Tom Pacey's partner, gave me the job.

On the strength of it I left home (by now I was living with Rosa, my real mother) and took a tiny basement flat at Stanhope Gate, near Marble Arch. The rent was as much as my pay and to make enough to live on I worked five nights a week stripping ceilings and scraping off old wallpaper for a decorator whom I met when he came to paint Pacey's office.

It was at this time that I met the man with the five-legged sheep and then – in the summer months at least – I was running three jobs.

I gave up my labouring and freak show side-lines just before I was sixteen when Tom Pacey set me to 'carrying a book'.

In show business parlance that meant that I had a small

notebook with the names of our agency's acts on one side and a space for each week of the year on the other. Whenever I had any spare time I would visit theatre bookers and try to fill the blank weeks with engagements.

My main job, however, was booking acts for Friday evenings. About fifty cinemas around London used to employ variety acts, a double and two singles, on Fridays as a special attraction. It was known as 'cine-variety' and the double act got three pounds and the singles thirty shillings each.

Tom Pacey controlled the variety bookings of thirty of these cinemas, so we had to find ninety acts a week.

Every night I toured the music halls, looking for acts. Pacey sometimes came with me and taught me how to value them. I was just a boy, but I was working on the same level as men. My confidence grew and so did my ability and earning power. Soon the commissions I earned from cine-variety more than made up for the money I had lost by giving up my part-time jobs.

After two and a half years I left Pacey to work for a firm which sold stationery. Again I worked on commission, selling paper and pencils to insurance companies and the many theatrical offices I knew.

But six months with the paper and pencils was long enough. I took an offer from Jack Doyle, the singing Irish heavyweight boxer. Jack had taken to the boards when he left the ring and with Charlie Forsyth, of the famous variety act Forsyth, Seaman and Farrel, he opened a variety agency.

At the Doyle and Forsyth office I worked with a man named Charles Harvard. Charles specialised in booking circus acts. He was older than I and because I probably needed a father figure at the time I turned to him. We decided to chance our arms and open our own agency and, with the blessing of Doyle and Forsyth, we left.

A meat packer called Archie Shenburn fancied himself as a show business tycoon and put some of his money into touring revues. Charles Harvard and I landed the job of booking and casting them.

I was seventeen years old and the youngest theatrical agent in London.

I was also on the side of the entertainment industry, that seemed pre-destined for me. Against the 'straight' theatre, variety has always been known as the 'illegitimate' end of the business.

What better place for a bastard...

ACT ONE
Scene 1: Sid James

He had a face like an unmade bed and a public image and personality that was the very embodiment of his battered, world weary and ungainly figure.

Sidney James was one of the best-loved entertainers ever to find acceptance from the British public and part of the secret of their affection for him was that to that all-important creature 'the man in the street', he was one of them.

And because in the type of character he portrayed he displayed so many of the qualities, and handicaps, that were so often part of them and their lives he earned the love of their womenfolk too.

For more than fourteen years I, too, loved Sid James. He was my client and my mate. But I knew the true being behind that image, a man who in almost every way was the total antithesis to what his adoring audience saw and took to their hearts.

The real Sid James was not, for a start, the dilapidated, slightly seamy rogue he so often played. In a profession where being well-dressed can approach the obsessional he could have won awards for his stylishness.

Sid had a wardrobe worth a fortune, upwards of two hundred of the finest suits, countless shirts and pairs of shoes and all the trappings to accompany them.

The cost of all this to Sid was precisely NOTHING!

From the moment that stardom came to Sid James he cashed in on it in every possible way, and that remarkable wardrobe was the best example of it.

His public saw him and accepted him as a carefree,

spendthrift character generally scheming to get hold of some quick and easy money to spend on a fruitless chase after romance, but in reality (and much as I loved and respected Sid as a human being, I must get this straight) he made Scrooge look like a public benefactor.

All those beautiful suits were the results of cunning contractual clauses Sid insisted I write into every deal I made for him.

If a film or stage part called for him to have a number of changes of clothes Sid would demand that the suits were made by Cyril Castle, at that time 'tailor by appointment to show business', and when the job was over the James wardrobe would benefit.

'I know you'll fix the right money for the part,' he would say, 'but what about the clobber?'

And if, God forbid, he had to wear his own clothes for a quick job like a TV commercial, Sid would still find a way of getting something on the side.

His favourite drink, or at least it became his favourite drink because it was free, was Cutty Sark whisky. For long periods in his life he received a case of the stuff a week... for mentioning the brand name of the booze on stage and demanding that it be included in the programme credits.

Sid did more than a dozen plays, from Britain to New Zealand, while I managed him and in every one of them he got those golden words 'Cutty Sark' into the script somewhere.

As a life-long Scotch drinker I had to admire the man, but I do wish he had preferred another brand, for every time I called on him at home I had to carry my own bottle. His 'hand-outs' were one tipple I couldn't take.

Sidney James came into my life one afternoon in the office of one of the most powerful men in British show business, Lord Delfont (although in those days he was plain, but still powerful, Bernard Delfont).

I was a director of the Bernard Delfont Agency, looking after the lives of people like Dick Emery and the 'Carry On' stars Kenneth Connor and Charles Hawtrey.

Bernard and I were talking business when he received a

telephone call from Sid, telling him that he was changing his management and could Bernard suggest anybody.

Bernard cupped his hand over the telephone mouthpiece and asked me: 'How do you fancy handling Sid James?'

I accepted immediately and the following day I went to his home in Ealing, West London.

There I met his wife, Valerie, a beautiful blonde in her thirties who was to become a major force in Sid's life, but at that first meeting I was more concerned with getting to know the man, not his wife.

The first thing I did learn about my new client was that he was in trouble. Big trouble.

In the sitting room of his home he showed me an architect's drawings of a new house he was having built at Iver, in Buckinghamshire. To me it looked like the design for a prison block, but I was trying to get a new client for the agency and made all the right complimentary noises.

'This is the new place we're having built,' said Sid, obviously in love with the thought of moving to Parkhurst in the countryside. 'It's costing a hundred and fifty grand and you'll be the guy who'll get me the work to pay for it.'

Then came the 'tag line', that timely pay-off so indispensable to every comic.

'Incidentally, I owe the tax people thirty five thousand. Can you get me out of that, too?'

In those days, the early Nineteen Sixties, £35,000 was the sort of money NOBODY owed to the tax man. The shock to my hardened system was so profound that I took a tube train back to the office instead of my usual taxi. Someone, somehow, had to start economising!

It may sound paradoxical that someone as mean as I soon learned Sid to be, should have been in such financial straits, but the other side of his nature was that he was the most profligate – and unlucky – gambler I have ever met.

Sid James made money his god, he would go to the most extraordinary lengths to get it, but left to his own devices he could never hold on to it.

Casinos, their roulette wheels and card tables held no joys

for Sid. After all, you can't work and gamble at the tables. But horses and dogs race somewhere just about every weekday of the year and bookmakers are always available at the end of a telephone.

I never knew a day to pass when Sid did not have a bet, and there was never a week when he finished ahead of the bookies.

His stakes were always in the hundreds of pounds and when the weekly day of reckoning came round it was a question of who got to me first: Sid or the bookies. Whoever it was the subject was always the same... money.

The day after I agreed to become his manager I got my first taste of Sid's gambling mania. He was working on a BBC-TV series 'Taxi!' in which he played a London cab driver called Sid. During a break in rehearsals at the BBC studios in Shepherds Bush, West London, he telephoned my office:

'Mick, do you think you can get over here? There's something I want to talk about. Something I need done.'

At the studios I found an agitated Sid. 'It's like this Mick, I've got these heavies coming round and there's nothing for them. Nothing!' His voice, naturally gruff and husky, had a ring of hysteria to it.

'Heavies? What do you mean heavies?'

'What I mean is that I owe them, they want it and if they don't get it they're going to take it out on me.'

Rapidly the panic-stricken Sid explained his gambling debts. He owed a bookmaker £600 and a couple of minders were on their way to collect.

So far I hadn't collected one penny in commission from my new client, but if I didn't do something soon I wouldn't have a client fit enough to earn commission from.

I went back to my office in the West End and took all the petty cash I could find. I added money of my own and returned to the studios where the receptionist told me: 'Mr Sullivan, there are two gentlemen waiting to see you.'

The pair sitting in the corner of the foyer hardly merited the description, but in spite of their looks they behaved civilly enough, especially when I pulled out the money.

'I believe it's all there fellers. Six hundred, O.K.?'

'No chum. You're wrong.'

Wrong? Now it was my turn to worry that they might take little bits off me to make up for what was still owing.

'It's five hundred. That's all we've come for.'

Totally bemused by this turn of events I peeled £100 off the roll, waited while they counted out the rest and politely saw them to the door.

Minutes later I was in the rehearsal room with Sid, explaining that he had miscalculated and was, in fact, £100 better off than he thought he was.

That creased, craggy face broke into the merest smile and he stuck out his hand. 'That's nice Mick. I could do with that.'

'Hold on, Sid. I just paid your debts. That other hundred isn't yours. It's got to go back to the office,' I told him.

'They can't need it that much mate, but I do.'

Like a clap of thunder the truth hit me. Sid had known all along just how much he owed his bookie. He had simply added an extra £100 to the amount so that he would have enough for another bet!

Out-wheeled and out-dealed I handed it over. That day I learned my first lesson in dealing with Sidney James and vowed never to fall for the same stroke again.

But I did, again and again. And so did many many other people he worked with and for.

If Sid owed a gambling debt of, say, £750 he would approach one of his buddies for a £1,000 loan. Of that £750 would pay for the horses that had lost and the remaining £250 was for those that were going to lose.

It took Valerie, his wife, quite a time to discover her husband's extravagant vice and when she did she cracked down upon him with a ferocity that left him reeling.

A limited company, Sidney James (Arts) was set up with Valerie and an accountant as the only directors. All of Sid's fees were paid into the firm and she allowed him just £5 a week pocket money. As inflation and his earnings grew Valerie showed the truly generous side of her nature... and increased it to £10.

Sidney accepted these restraints with a surprising equanimity. He played the good, dutiful husband to perfection and Valerie told me with glowing pride how he would sit at home on Saturday afternoons watching racing on TV and ringing his bookmaker with 'five shillings each way' on this horse or another.

If I had liked her enough I could have felt sorry for her, but Val's non-stop interference in my daily life with telephone calls querying the most petty contractual points and demands for accounting on the smallest and most inessential items had not endeared her to me. She was playing the part of the leading director of Sidney James Arts to the hilt and I just let her get on with it.

I kept my silence and, along with the wily Sid, shared the joke.

Those 'five shilling' bets were part of a code he had agreed with his bookie. For 'shilling' read 'one hundred pounds', and when the bet went down, as it inevitably did, Sid found the money to pay up.

He was not only an expert at getting his clothes and his whisky for free. He also got hold of plenty of hard cash by the simple expedient of taking part of his fees – even from film parts – in cash.

If Sid were asked to perform a shop opening or make a TV commercial, the fee stipulated on the contract was only part of the deal. The rest came in cash.

The money came in, and went out... to his bookmakers... and he even managed to wheedle money out of that limited company to keep pace with his gambling losses.

He would tell Val, for instance, that a dresser or make-up artist he had working for him was costing twice as much as the man was really getting and Val, convinced that she was dealing with a reformed character, would pay up.

With earnings of £3,000 and more each week, Sid kept alive the myth that he could get by on his pittance of pocket money, but all the time he was plunging deeper into debt.

Burdened with that £35,000 income tax bill for a start, he was forever running round in financial circles and catching his own tail, never quite managing to stay ahead of his debts. He should have died a wealthy man, but the only riches he left behind him were in the memories of the millions he had made laugh over the years.

I walked into Sid's career as he was making 'Taxi!', and for him I negotiated his contracts for TV classics like 'Bless This House' and 'George And The Dragon'. He appeared in pantomime at the London Palladium for me and toured Britain, South Africa, Australia and New Zealand in plays.

To the public I suppose that Sid James will always fall into the classification 'comedian', but in the strictest sense of the word he was never a comic. Sid was an actor, an excrutiatingly funny one, but he was totally lost when it came to playing the solo funny man.

He couldn't even tell a joke in a bar and if he wanted to raise a laugh over a drink he would give me a prod with: 'Tell 'em that one about... Mick.'

His amazing meanness had its funny side and I often laugh when I recall the lengths he would go to in order to save – and make – money. In the years we were together I never knew him to buy a car. He would take one from a manufacturer or distributor as his payment for making public appearances or appearing in TV commercials, and more than once the car was immediately sold. Four legs meant far more than four wheels to Sid.

He would demand first class air tickets to get to and from an engagement in the North of England... and then cash in the ticket and drive to the date. The money, as always, paid his gambling debts.

A startling example of Sid's tight-fistedness took place, of all times, one Christmas. He had arranged a party and among the guests was comedian Jack Douglas, whom I also managed.

Jack, an old friend of Sid's, was starring in pantomime at Wimbledon, near London, and by the time he had got off stage, taken his make-up off, changed and driven to Sid's Buckinghamshire home the party had been going for some hours.

Jack, with his wife Sue, walked in the front door about two minutes after midnight. Mine host Sid wished them both a Merry Christmas, kissed Sue and asked what they would like to drink.

'Champagne would be great, old son', said Jack, having noticed that many of the 40 or so guests (including my wife Dany and myself) were drinking the stuff.

'Sorry mate. There's none left,' said Sidney. 'What about some white wine instead?'

I couldn't believe this. There had been champagne a-plenty and it couldn't all have gone.

It hadn't, but Sid had decided that, in the interests of economy, the expensive boozing would stop at midnight. And Jack and Sue were just two minutes too late!

Jack settled for the white wine and the pay-off came a few days later when Sid called me:

'Mick, do you remember the champagne I got in for the party? Well, I've got six cases left over. D'you think someone in the office can take it back to the supplier and get me a refund?'

That was Sidney James, but in spite of it all he was a joy to be with.

When Sid decided to install that star status symbol, a heated swimming pool, at his home in Iver the undertaking became a major financial project. All sorts of quotes for the work were garnered by him and Valerie, contractors driven mad as corners were cut to save money... and eventually the pool, as imaginative and attractive as the fortress-like house it graced was ready for use.

But Sidney was away so often for the first three years after the pool arrived that he never had a chance to use it.

The pool had been forgotten by Sid's friends until one day he started making phone calls to everybody: 'How much does it cost to heat a swimming pool?' It had to be the daftest question in the world and nobody was interested in the cost of hot swimming water anyway.

Unable to find out exactly how much his first dip would cost, Sid went ahead and switched on the heating system for the pool. It was mid-June, warm, and the water needed just a touch of extra heat to make swimming tolerable.

What he had not bargained for was that, in his desperate attempts to save money wherever possible, he had installed 'definitely the cheapest heating system in the world'. It may have been cheap but it was too effective. The pool was linked to the oil-fired central heating for the house (this was in the days before OPEC went mad with prices) and would only operate if the heating for the house was working at the same time.

There was no way to turn radiators off in individual rooms and the James family came home in the evening and sweltered in 98 degrees of heat!

At one stage when Sid's gambling began to worry even me I asked him: 'Why do you do it? You must know that in the long run you can't come out a winner and with your luck there's no long run. You lose EVERY time'.

There was not a moment's hesitation before he stunned me with: 'I just love losing, Mick. To me it's like having an orgasm.'

I suppose that everyone has the right to get their sexual gratification in the way they want, but throwing his money at bookmakers wasn't Sid's only way.

He was, without doubt, one of the randiest human beings I have ever met. In the entertainment profession there are always opportunities for a little illicit loving and the rampant Sid took full advantage of them.

With that ex-boxer's face and a voice like a bulldozer in distress, he wasn't anyone's idea of a romantic figure, but that never stopped him and his success with women was phenomenal.

No girl, in any film, TV show or play that he ever performed in was safe from his charm, and generally he got lucky.

These romances never developed into long-running affairs. They never reached the level of 'one night stands'. For Sid they were more like 'lunch break stands'.

At Pinewood studios, just three miles from his home, Sid rarely showed up in the bar for a lunch-time drink, and never (unless I arrived to take him for lunch) ate in the studio restaurant. Valerie sent her ever-loving off to work each day with a packed sandwich lunch which he ate in his dressing room.

What she didn't realise was that those packed lunches were an ideal excuse for Sid to stay locked away for an hour in the middle of the day 'resting'. And there was generally somebody soft to share the time with.

Gerald Thomas and Peter Rogers, the director and producer of the 'Carry On' movies, would notice that one of their younger and more attractive small part players was missing at lunch time and accept the fact resignedly.

'At least we'll have two happy members of the cast at work this afternoon,' they would agree.

Only one of Sid's affairs ever reached the proportions of a full-blown romance and it took a long, long time to come to fruition, but when it did Sid fell hopelessly in love.

The girl was busty, blonde Cockney actress Barbara Windsor who had worked with Sid on almost every 'Carry On' film but had never been one of his lunch-time ladies.

In fact, although they were great mates, it was not until they appeared in 'Carry On London', a stage version of the films which was to run for 15 months at Victoria Palace Theatre, London, in 1971 and 1972, that the romance took off.

The production was rehearsed for four weeks in Birmingham and opened there at the Hippodrome Theatre for a two week trial run.

Sid, as I have said, was a funny actor, not a stand up comic. He was never at home facing a theatre audience working a sketch or telling gags, and that was what the show called for.

He would work himself into a very nervous state and endanger everything.

Barbara, on the other hand, with her background of night club and theatre work in revues knew just how to cope with this sort of work and it was she who took Sid by the hand during rehearsals and helped him.

They were both out of London, living in the same hotel and with plenty of spare time in the evenings. It was inevitable that the friendship should develop.

It did and it lasted for the full run of the show.

Sid rented a flat in Dolphin Square, a huge block by the Thames at Victoria, telling Valerie that he couldn't cope with the drive home to Buckinghamshire every night. The real reason was to be with Barbara during the days. Their romance became an open secret and I had to warn him about his indiscretion:

'What you're doing is all over London, Sid. Everybody in the business knows about it. What happens if the Press get hold of it?'

'I couldn't care less about the Press,' said Sid. 'I am madly in love with the girl.'

The affair went on and at one time I was convinced that Sid was ready to throw up everything and marry Barbara. But somehow Valerie found out about it. That and the fact that the show came to an end in turn brought Sid to his senses and an end to the romance.

The show closed in November 1972 and Sid came to my home on the El Paraiso golf course at Marbella in Southern Spain for a short holiday before Valerie arrived and they moved into a nearby hotel together.

A few days after he arrived I had to travel to Barcelona and as I left the house he asked me to do a favour for him.

'Send a dozen roses to Barbara, will you Mick. Put in a card and sign it "Romeo".'

Romeo! Nobody with a face like Sid's could possibly be serious about that. But he was, and he had shown that the affair was continuing in spite of the trouble it had caused between him and Valerie.

I sent the roses as I stopped off in Marbella on my drive to Malaga airport for the flight to Barcelona. On the way I mused over Sid's amorous nature and had a private laugh over the problems it caused him.

But there was no stopping Romeo James. I had always known that, and it was a full six months later when I really learned just how all-powerful Sid's lust was.

For while I was away on that trip to Barcelona. He tried to make love to my wife. Not once. But twice. My client, my friend, in my house, trying to 'make' my wife!

Dany told me about it after making me promise that I would not lose my temper, do anything drastic or even confront Sid about it.

'On the night you left I took Sid to a party at the home of a friend. We got back around three, said goodnight to each other in the sitting room. He went to the guest room and I went to our bedroom,' she said.

'I was asleep when I heard this mumbling. I turned on my side and there was Sid, kneeling at the side of the bed. I thought he was drunk and praying and had lost his way. Then I woke up fully and heard him asking: 'Come on Dany, what about it?'

Dany apparently kept her temper, told Sid that he must be out of his mind and ordered him to go to his own room. Sheepishly he did so.

The next morning they breakfasted together and Dany, determined not to raise the matter, talked about the weather, golf and swimming.

It took Sid a full two hours to blurt out his apology.

'Dany, about last night. I can't tell you how sorry I am. I must have been drunk out of my skull. I'm just so sorry. Please forgive and please don't tell Mick. We've been friends for so long it would ruin everything.'

Dany, whose affection for Sid was on par with my own, told him to forget the whole thing and promised she would not mention the incident to me.

But the following night Sid tried again. And this time Dany woke up to find him in bed next to her. What followed was an encore of the previous night and the next day the flood of apologies started again.

Dany kept her word and said nothing about it to me until one night when we were discussing Sid and something he had done which caused me a lot of extra work and irritated Dany but not me.

'I'll tell you about your precious Sid,' yelled Dany... and out came the story of his nocturnal wandering.

There can be only two reactions to news of that sort: either you want to kill the man or you laugh.

I laughed and then began to wonder about the supreme egotism of the man who would be prepared to try again after such a rebuff and after making such a fool of himself.

I was away from Marbella for just two days, but I am sure if I hadn't been there on the third night Sid would have tried again. He always believed in backing outsiders!

Sid James died because he would not stop working. Of that there is no question.

He should have realised the chances he was taking after suffering a first massive heart attack at his home.

Sid had finished recording the very last episode of his TV comedy series 'George And The Dragon' at the ATV studios in Elstree, Hertfordshire. I had been there for the show and after a few drinks we drove home – me to Denham and Sid to his house which was three or four miles away.

At two in the morning my telephone rang. On the end of the line was Valerie James: 'Can you get here right away, Michael,' she said. 'Sid's had a heart attack.'

I drove to the house in Iver. A doctor was already there and Sid was lying, in his pyjamas, unconscious on a couch in the sitting room.

The doctor had been on the telephone trying to arrange an ambulance to take Sid to a heart hospital in King's Cross in the centre of London. However the local ambulance service could only operate within its own area and he had been told to contact London and get an ambulance from there.

'There just isn't time, or at least I'm not going to chance it,' he said. 'Do you think you could drive him to the hospital? I'll go ahead in my car and arrange everything, but you must not travel at more than 25 miles an hour. Will you do it?'

Between us Val, the doctor and I carried Sid to my car, a heavy sedate Austin Van Den Plas with a Rolls Royce engine. The 27 mile journey that followed was the longest and most nerve-wracking of my life.

I kept well below the doctor's 25 miles an hour limit because I thought that even the slightest bump could endanger the life of Sid, who lay unconscious wrapped in blankets on the back seat.

Sid spent the next three weeks in an oxygen tent at the hospital and another three in a ward. He begged the doctors to let him go home and when they did he stayed in a ground floor room for three months, forbidden to attempt to climb the stairs.

It took a further three months to recuperate and he was allowed to return to work only after he promised that he would not exert himself.

Sid kept his promises... for a while. But little by little he took on more work and began to drink more.

When I tackled him about his drinking which had been on the increase and told him that with his heart condition whisky was not the best medicine he looked at me for a while and said very quietly:

'Mick, I want you to know something. I don't give a fuck.'

'You mean you don't care if you die?'

'That's it mate.'

'Sid, are you that unhappy?'

'Yes, that unhappy.'

I never found out just what the tragedy that lay in the heart of this great clown was. It was one secret Sid would not share with me.

Apart from that one incident he was very much the same person, working, womanising and gambling, cheating on Val over money and girls, until the night he died.

The end came in classic, corny show business tradition, four years after his heart attack, on the stage of the Empire Theatre, Sunderland, on his opening night in a play 'The Mating Season' which had been especially written for Sid by Sam Cree.

At 8.45 pm during the first act one of the cast Olga Lowe 'fed' Sid a line as he sat on a settee. He did not reply, but just sat there. Olga spoke her lines again. This time she realised something was wrong. She ran off stage and the curtains were closed.

Sidney James, aged 63, had died... still trying to make people laugh.

I was called at my home in Marbella and flew to England. Three days after his death Sid was buried in a Jewish cemetery at Golders Green, North London.

The place was packed. Half of the British entertainment industry seemed to be there, as well as hundreds of his fans who waited silently in the early winter sunshine.

Louis Benjamin, boss of the London Palladium, delivered a tribute to Sid and we left the cemetery Val James gripped my arm and said: 'Aren't there a lot of people here.'

I helped her into her car and replied: 'Sid always played to a full house, love.'

Scene Two: Errol Flynn

There was no town in the whole wide world like Tijuana in the late Nineteen Forties and early Fifties. The dust hole just a step over the Mexican border from California lived on vice and for vice.

Enough money (and you didn't need that much) could buy you anything you wanted, with anybody you wanted, and any way you wanted it.

With its whoring, boozing, cock-fighting, gambling and brawling it was a hell-fire preacher's vision of eternal damnation brought to earthly life.

It was my idea of a fun place to be if you were drunk enough.

For Errol Flynn it was a spiritual home.

The greatest certainty on this earth was that the town and man should come together. Tijuana was tailor-made for Flynn, the Hollywood action king with the looks and build of a god and the mind of a lecherous imp.

It was a fair bet that I, too, should discover the delights of Tijuana, and after my first visit there with Nico Minardos, a Greek actor friend from Hollywood, I couldn't wait to return.

I made it alone a week after the trip with Nico in the summer of 1949. I was in Hollywood scouting talent for Eric Maschwitz, then head of light entertainment for BBC Television and the man who wrote that wonderful war-time song 'A Nightingale Sang In Berkeley Square'.

Any nightingale I was likely to find in Tijuana was bound to be a bit scruffy around the tail feathers, but I had the needs of the British Broadcasting Corporation far, far from my mind when I tumbled into my nineteenth (or was it twenty-ninth?) bar.

Trouble wasn't around the next corner in Tijuana. It was right next to you. All you had to do was turn around and walk into it.

I did just that when the drunk at the bar next to me leaned on me too heavily once too often. As I turned to him I warned: 'If you do that once more...'

Then I managed to focus for a moment. The drunk was all of six feet two inches tall, stacked like one of those adverts for body-building equipment, and so handsome it hurt.

'Mr Flynn, do accept my apologies,' I grovelled. 'I didn't recognise you.' In the Sullivan book there are better ways of getting out of trouble than with a batch of broken bones.

Flynn laughed and the guy at his side laughed too, the most infectious laugh I have ever heard. I learned very soon after that the voice that went with the laugh was pretty special too, but at the moment I was too busy laughing with them. I was out of trouble and wanted to stay that way.

'Let's have a drink', I suggested.

'Let's', said Flynn who introduced himself and his friend, Dick Haymes, the American singer who even Frank Sinatra bowed to when it came to phrasing a slow ballad.

That brush in a Mexican bar lead to a friendship with Flynn that spanned ten years. As we drank we discovered that we had a number of things in common: we were all in show business, we were all half-Irish and we had all had three wives.

After a few drinks Flynn was ready to move on. 'We're going to a strip show, fancy coming along?' he asked. 'It might be interesting. It's something different.'

'Different. How different?'

'All the broads are pregnant'.

In my business it never hurts to see a new attraction and, after all, I was scouting talent for BBC Television!

We stayed for just one act of the show in the bar across the road. It was, we all agreed, a humiliating, revolting experience and we needed a drink to wash away the memory.

Dawn came and we parted. Flynn and Dick Haymes to the star's beloved yacht *Sirocco* and me to drive back to Hollywood.

'I'd stay for a few more, but I don't want to risk being picked up by the cops with this amount of booze inside me,' I mumbled. 'Do you know a decent hotel?'

They hooted with laughter. 'In Tijuana? Forget it. Do what Rich and I do,' said Flynn.

'What's that?'

'Get arrested and stay in the local jail. It's clean, comfortable and...'

Haymes cut in: '... and you'll have fun.'

'Are you serious?'

'So serious that if we didn't have a tide to catch we'd join you'.

I watch them leave and sensed that they were having me on. But, then, their response to my question had come without a second's hesitation that to my muddled, fuzzy mind it seemed that they might just have something.

What the hell! I'd been in jail before. I got into my car and drove it straight into a lamp-post and within seconds a patrolling police car had arrived. I was hauled out from the driving seat, and after one of the two Mexican cops had taken my keys and reversed my car off the wooden sidewalk and parked it on the roadside, I was whisked off to the police station.

Once there I was stripped down to my underpants, shakily wrote my name in the register and hustled into a cell.

By now I was beginning to sober up and I started to take stock of the place.

I sat on a well-sprung cot and in the corner was a toilet with a piece of cord instead of a chain, a roll of paper and – sitting on the edge of a stained wash basin – a small hand towel, clean and ironed with a broken piece of soap.

About ten minutes passed and by now I was sprawled on the cot, hands behind my head, looking at the ceiling and recalling Dick Haymes' remark:

'You'll have fun'.

Some fun! I should have known the whole thing was a gag.

I had started to laugh at myself when a hefty guard beckoned me to the iron bars and spoke in fractured English:

'You look. You pick. I get'.

Through the bars he handed a piece of folded cardboard and I returned to my bunk and opened what I can describe as a pleasure menu. There were pictures of half a dozen girls with their measurements, names and prices together with very graphic descriptions of their 'specialities'.

The most expensive was Juanita and, for obvious safety and hygienic reasons, I chose her. Seventy-five American dollars was a lot of money in those days, but she was enchanting and exciting.

After the main event we rested until the morning sun was high, high above and the jailer arrived and opened the cell door.

Juanita escorted me to the jail entrance where I collected my clothes and a scruffy piece of paper on which was scribbled:

Juanita	$75
Extra towel	$15
Gratuity	$25
Car park	$25
TOTAL	$140

My jailer pointed to my money, deducted the amount and then showed me through the door.

As I left with Juanita to find the car I suddenly stopped, returned to the desk with her and asked to translate:

'Do I have to get arrested, or can I pop in any time?'

She quickly provided the answer. It was very necessary to get arrested. Otherwise it just WASN'T LEGAL!

As I drove back to L.A. I reflected on it all. Flynn was absolutely right. It was certainly the best hotel in town. And it had the prettiest maid service!

Before we parted Flynn and I made arrangements to meet in Hollywood and about a fortnight later I telephoned him at Cirrhosis-By-The-Sea, the name his cronies gave to his Malibu Beach home.

In Tijuana we had talked about fencing and Errol had described how much help and coaching he had been given by Basil Rathbone, the English actor who played Sherlock Holmes to such perfection in so many films.

Rathbone, who died eight years ago in his eighties, was a great swordsman in real life and during our telephone conversation Errol mentioned that he was visiting him the following day (a Sunday) and invited me along.

'If you're that interested in fencing I'll get Basil to give you a lesson while we're there.'

Basil Rathbone lived in a pseudo-Tudor house on an estate in Bel-Air. It was like being in Sunningdale, Berkshire, and the furniture and fittings of the place reflected the very Englishness of its owner.

Flynn had picked me up at my hotel and driven me to Bel-Air. After being introduced to Rathbone's wife Errol and I sat with our host on a terrace by the garden swimming pool.

Over the drinks Errol raised the subject of fencing and Basil suggested 'a parry or two' on the lawn.

I had seen the pair of them fight those epic film duels in 'Captain Blood' and 'The Adventures Of Robin Hood' and thrilled to them... and now here they were, hero and arch villain, putting a show with me as the only audience.

To a background of a recording of Tchaikovsky's opera 'Romeo and Juliet' – chosen by Basil because he found it 'ideal fencing music' – they parried and thrust at each for about 15 minutes, with Basil, nearly twenty years Errol's senior, showing his superior skill with every movement.

After watching the two masters of cinema swordmanship I was invited by Basil to take part in a short session.

'We'll do it the way we do it in films,' he said.

'By numbers'.

He explained that every position was given a number and after we had rehearsed about half a dozen of them he would call 'two', 'six', 'three' as he made his thrust. All I did was stick the foil in the right position and it looked as though I'd been leaping around battlements all my life.

My next meeting with Errol was in London's Dorchester Hotel. He was in Britain to make a film for producer-director

Herbert Wilcox and they were lunching together at the time.

He invited me to Pinewood studios to watch the shooting of the movie 'Lilacs In The Spring' and told me: 'I've got myself into trouble again, old sport.'

It happened on the first day of filming. Flynn had been called for make-up at 7.30 a.m. He never showed and an entire film crew sat around waiting until mid-day when our hero arrived on the set – followed by half a dozen waiters, each with a case of champagne on their shoulders. Flynn had decided to turn the first day into a party.

'I thought "fuck the filming" dear boy. Let's have a party and start the whole thing off with a bit of fun,' he said. 'Herbert was not amused. Can't think why.'

It was the measure of the man that he genuinely couldn't understand why Wilcox failed to see the joy of the occasion, but then Errol never stopped for a moment to consider that all of those people on the set had to be paid for wasting time.

In the middle of one week he telephoned my office and asked what I was doing at the week-end. We agreed to meet at Pinewood at the end of filming on the Friday.

'I'll have the studio car,' said Errol, 'so come by taxi. We might have a drink or two.'

By the time I reached the panelled bar in the huge stately house that forms the office block of the studios 'Flynski' was in full song.

'Let's go on a pub crawl,' he suggested. 'But not London. People will come up and ask me for autographs and things like that and, just for once, I don't want to be bothered.

'I think we should go to Cardiff.'

'Cardiff!' I screamed. 'Do you have any frigging idea how far that is?'

Flynski (this had became my drinking name for him) was unruffled. 'I know how far it is, sport, but there are lots of pubs on the way and those Welsh birds are something else.'

A few drinks later, chauffered by a terrific Cockney driver called Alf who had been ordered by Flynn to remove his cap ('I can't stand all this uniform bullshit') we were on our way to Cardiff... via a score of pubs and a few score drinks.

The 'something else' Errol was looking for turned up in strength in Cardiff's Tiger Bay dock area, one of the roughest, toughest parts of Britain. There were four of them, two white and two black, none of them pretty, but all eager and *very* professional.

Flynn summed up the situation the moment we were all settled in a bar. 'What are we going to do with this lot, sport. Fuck or play dominoes?'

I was in no condition to play anything and when Flynski disappeared with his two companions I paid my pair off and staggered to the room in the small hotel whose owner had been daft, or drunk, enough to allow us to stay the night.

Errol's great love, which I believe took precedence over women and boozing, was his boat – or rather boats. During the time I knew him he owned two: *Sirocco* and *Zaca*, a beautiful black-hulled schooner that took a crew of about ten to sail and maintain.

He was always wealthy enough to live the high life and on *Zaca* he managed to combine it with the freedom he had sought for so long.

Very much a 'man's man', he was never happier than when he was at sea and it was because of his love of travel and *Zaca* that we met again in Majorca.

The Mediterranean island had been a watering hole for both him and me for years, but we were never there at the same time until the mid-Fifties.

We met through a mutual friend, the old Hollywood actor Paul Lukas, who lived on the island until his death in 1971, and over a drink Flynski suggested we should re-live some old times.

'Haymes and I are taking *Zaca* to Jamaica in November,' he said. 'Why don't you meet us there?'

I stole five days off from the office to go to the West Indies and every one of those days seemed like a life-time. Dick Haymes, Flynn and I lived aboard *Zaca*, but the schooner never once lifted anchor. The only boat trips we took were by dinghy to and from Kingston harbour to get us to the bars and back again.

Flynn's reputation as an actor – not as a drunk – carried plenty of clout on Jamaica and he had been invited to an official garden party thrown by the British governor of the island.

'We're all going', announced Captain Flynn to first and second mates Haymes and Sullivan.

'On your own,' chorused the mutinous pair. 'Who needs all that?'

Flynn insisted, he cajoled and wheedled and finally we gave in. I had to go ashore to buy some decent clothes for the big bunfight and we left for the party.

An hour of being polite to the local dignitaries was all that Flynn could take. 'We're going,' he said. 'Ready?'

We made our farewells, took the dinghy back to *Zaca*, changed into our drinking gear and returned to the bars of Kingston.

No one will ever know what time we got back to *Zaca* the following morning. Nobody cared. But whatever the time Flynn was in a hurry. On the tour of the bars he had picked up a black lady who must have weighed all of 18-stone and her ugliness was in direct proportion to her poundage.

Dick Haymes and I immediately disappeared to our cabins on *Zaca*. Haymes was too drunk to stay awake. I was too drunk and too worn out from having to row the pair of us plus Flynn and his heavyweight back to the schooner.

Some time around mid-day Haymes and I emerged and went on deck for a 'livener'. Haymes had just tilted back his first vodka and tonic when across the blue waters a small white launch chugged towards us.

'They're coming this way,' said Dick. 'By Christ, it's that governor guy and his daughter. That crazy bastard's invited them to visit.'

The next five minutes were spent clearing the bottles from the deck, rousing Flynn and telling him to hide his lady love. Racial equality wasn't exactly the norm on Jamaica in those days, particularly when the Governor was calling.

'Just hide her. Anywhere,' I pleaded with Flynn. 'If you have to, put her in the fridge.'

'The fridge?'

'Well, it's big enough and if she doesn't move around too much she'll keep for another time.'

Flynn strode off in mock disgust. Obviously he had plans of his own.

The Governor and his daughter were already on board when Flynn came on deck from his cabin. Dick Haymes and I had presented ourselves to our distinguished guests, seated them and given them drink.

Flynn looked immaculate in a blue silk tee-shirt, blue and white striped trousers and white shoes. How the man managed to look like that after the night he'd had staggered me.

But what shocked me more was what followed. All 18-stone of it!

Flynn, with all the dignity and aplomb of a career diplomat took her hand, led her forward and said to the Governor: 'Welcome aboard. How lovely of you to come. Now... have you met Mrs... SULLIVAN!'

Thankfully, over the years my mind has become a complete blank about what followed. And I want it to stay that way.

My final get-together with Errol Flynn took place in Paris in 1957. I had bought the TV rights of the Bulldog Drummond books and the only man who – to me – fitted the part of the so British hero created by 'Sapper' was my old mate Flynn. He had the looks, the accent, the ability and the drawing power to make a series based on the books a huge success.

I checked his whereabouts from the Celebrity Bulletin, a weekly 'who's where' sheet that most show business and media people subscribe to, and learned that he was staying in the Napoleon Hotel in Paris.

I booked a suite in the George V Hotel and flew to Paris, having first telephoned Errol and arranged to meet him at nine that evening at the Napoleon.

He had just finished filming 'The Sun Also Rises', based on the Ernest Hemingway novel 'Fiesta' – a story built around the annual bull fight festival in the Northern Spanish town of Pamplona.

Errol had a penthouse apartment at the hotel and a

beautiful young girl with him. He was tanned and looked fitter than I'd ever seen him.

I explained that I wanted him for the part of Bulldog Drummond and that I had enough money to make a 'pilot' programme.

'I played that part in a repertory theatre in Northampton before the war, old sport,' he said. 'But now. I'm not fit enough and I'm 48 years old. It needs a younger, fitter guy.'

I couldn't accept that and we sat down to drink and argue about the part. The faster the drink flowed the more intense the arguments became.

Errol wouldn't listen to reason – at least that's the way I saw it – and he picked me up by the seat of my pants, opened the door and dumped me in the hall.

I realised that I had left my raincoat behind and rapped on the door. It was answered by a straight to my left eye and followed by my raincoat which fell over me like a shroud as I hit the deck.

The door slammed and there was no point in pushing any more. Flynn, with the help of a lot of vodka, had made up his mind.

All I could do was yell at the door: 'I don't want you to play the part tonight!' and go back to my hotel.

The next morning I was nursing my black eye when, the door to my suite opened and a young waiter carrying a silver salver approached my bed. He lifted the cover of the dish to reveal a large raw fillet steak with a card attached to it. The card read:

'Do forgive me, old mate – Errol.'

That touching thought made me forget my anger with the man and it soon turned to laughter, because at intervals of five minutes another steak would arrive... and it went on until I had 36 of them scattered around the room, and with each one the attached message got funnier and funnier. The last one read:

'You've got enough flesh now. Build your own bulldog.'

I telephoned Errol and we made up our quarrel as he explained that he just did not feel fit enough to tackle an

Above my father, Sir Fredrick Allen, Chairman of P & O Liners. My mother, Rosa, at the Alhambra Theatre, London, in "The Bing Boys" and below Sir Arthur Sullivan of Gilbert and Sullivan fame, where the vein of our showbiz family began.

Sisters three: Rosa, Kit and Bid

A proud keepsake when my mother performed in the presence of their Majesties the King and Queen in 1916.

ENTERTAINMENTS TO WOUNDED SAILORS AND SOLDIERS
GIVEN BY, AND IN THE PRESENCE OF
THEIR MAJESTIES THE KING AND QUEEN
(IN THE RIDING SCHOOL)
AT
BUCKINGHAM PALACE
ON TUESDAY, WEDNESDAY & THURSDAY, MARCH 21, 22, 23, 1916

PALACE THEATRE, W.

March 31, 1916.

Dear Miss Rosie Sullivan,

His Majesty The King has graciously expressed the desire that I should convey to the artists who appeared at the above Entertainments his appreciation of their kindness in so doing, and of the excellence of every number presented.

I feel sure that you will be highly gratified by His Majesty's kindly thought, and I would like to add my personal thanks for your valuable co-operation.

Best Wishes,

Yours faithfully,

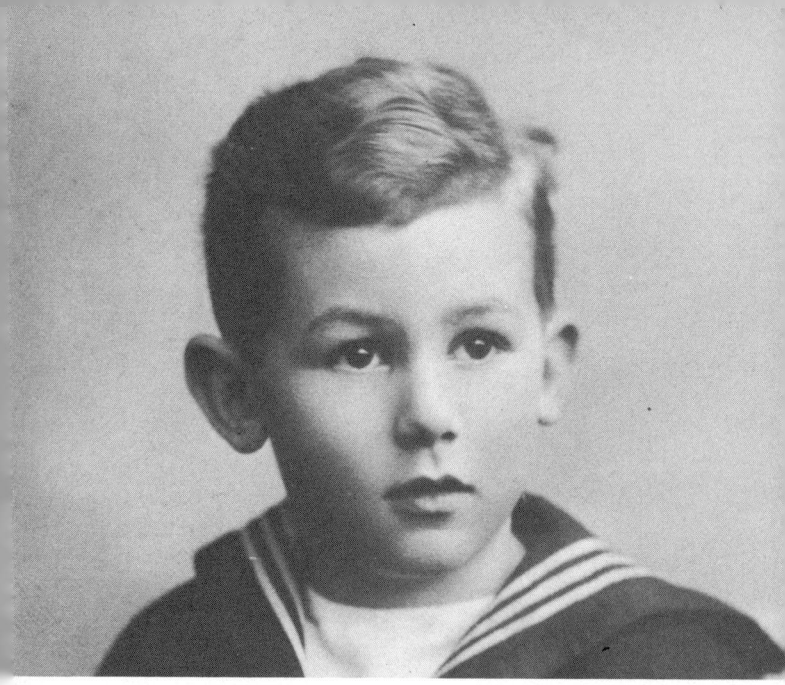

At the age of 6 already to sail the seven seas and the photograph that won me a seven year contract as an actor with Paramount Pictures in 1939. Right my dear sister Sheila.

Sid kissed my wife — was he kissing Dany or watching me? Jack Douglas deservedly kissed my bride for all the help he gave me in the arrangements for the wedding.

Carry on London — The last of the big spectacular reviews at the Victoria Palace.

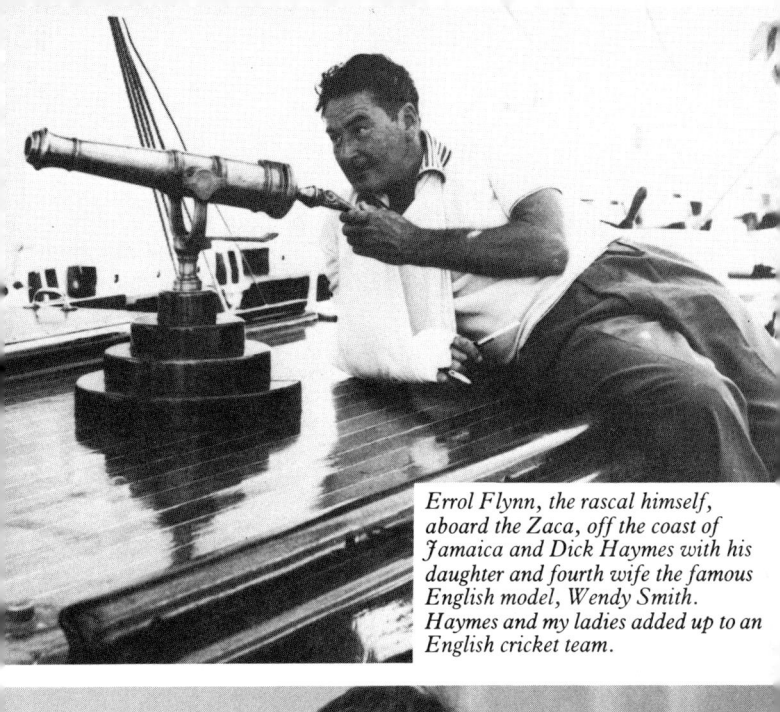

Errol Flynn, the rascal himself, aboard the Zaca, off the coast of Jamaica and Dick Haymes with his daughter and fourth wife the famous English model, Wendy Smith. Haymes and my ladies added up to an English cricket team.

Roger Moore, my favourite 007, who saved my life and Michael Parkinson who has such an eye for talent that he would have made a better agent than I.

arduous TV series, no matter how well he looked. I understood and after arranging to keep in touch I flew back to London.

Two years later Errol died in Montreal, Canada, and I was both happy and saddened to see him just three weeks before his death.

We met by chance at La Guardia Airport. I was on my way to California and he was flying to the country where – just a short time later – he would die.

The robust, hell-raising picture of health I knew so well from the past, looked an old and beaten man.

He leaned heavily on a stick, his complexion was a sickly mauve colour and his hair had turned white.

'What have you been doing to yourself Flynski?'

'I've been to Cuba. They've got some trouble down there and I got some shrapnel in my leg, old sport. You know me. Can't resist a bit of bother.'

We had no time for a drink together because his flight was being called. He limped off and gave me a hug and wink before he left. 'See you soon, old sport. Keep it up.'

Later in London I read of his death in Canada at the age of 50. A man burned out far before his time... but what a time he'd made of it.

Now that they are both dead there is one point I want to raise about Errol and David Niven, something that, in fairness to my old friend, should be recorded.

In Niven's early days in Hollywood Errol did his best to help him, knowing full well that his friend was – as actors go – very much a light weight.

It has always made me angry that in his books Niven devoted so much space to denigrating Errol in a patronising and condescending manner, even though it was under the guise of friendship.

My anecdotes will show, I hope, the deep affection I had for Flynn... a man who was an all-time winner both as a screen personality and a friend.

Scene Three: A Brush with the Stars

Every night in rooms all over the world a group of men – and a few women – offer up a rather extraordinary prayer before they go to sleep.

The languages they use and the object of their invocations vary with their countries and their faiths, but the sense of it is always the same.

They don't ask for money, power, beautiful mates, youth or everlasting life. Brought down to basic, simple English it comes to this:

'Please, please send me a star'.

These people are called agents.

The mystic symbol in their lives is the figure 'Ten Per Cent'. It represents what they call commission.

In all of the years that I was one of that maligned and abused band I, too, prayed for the day when my office door would open and my star would walk through it. Not a star already, but just a little twinkle willing and with the talent to be polished and burnished into a great big gleaming STAR.

I must have been kind to the right old ladies or washed behind my ears regularly because more than once that happened. But that is another part of this story.

My list of the big-timers I spotted and missed or started and then released before I realised their potential is as long as the next agent's, but I have had enough successes to be able to recall them without rancour.

Around 1950 I was trying to put together a touring show called 'Ice Fantasia'. Shifting an ice rink around the country involved one big problem: putting down the ice and freezing it every week at a new theatre.

I was convinced that it could be done and I discussed it with a man called Beresford Clarke, a former circus owner and property dealer who was backing my shows. 'Berry' eventually came up with a commercial method which, when adapted to our demands, could lay an ice rink in eight hours.

I had the rink and show... but no skaters. I started my search for a cast by going to Streatham Ice Rink in South London and asking around for likely girls.

I was given the name and address of one girl, attractive and good on the ice, who lived nearby in Brixton Hill. I went to see her to arrange an audition at the Streatham rink. While we were in her flat the door opened and a remarkably attractive man walked in.

'This is my husband, Roger. He's an actor. You can't do anything for him as well, can you?' said the pretty blonde.

I had a pantomime 'Dick Whittington' opening at the Brixton Empress that Christmas. One part required no talent, just the ability to look good.

'I can give you a little part as the Sultan in the second half of Dick Whittington. It's only one line and it pays twenty quid a week. Do you fancy it?'

He grabbed it and the first words Roger Moore ever uttered on stage were: 'Bring on the dancing girls.'

If I had known just how big a star Roger was destined to become I would have GIVEN him the girls, every one of them, for a chance of signing him to a contract.

We did, in fact, have a short-term contract between us a few years later when he was married to singer Dorothy Squires. I had booked Dot to play Prince Charming in another pantomime 'Cinderella' at the Tivoli Theatre, Hull, and she insisted on putting Roger, still a struggling actor, into the panto as the Baron.

After that Dot and Roger took off for California where that indefatigable woman turned her husband into a star. Dot, who has never understood the meaning of the word 'No' literally MADE Roger a screen name with her furious energy.

Whatever I may have considered Roger owed me for that early start was repaid a thousand fold when I visited Dot and him in Hollywood. They invited me to spend the day at their apartment at Westwood and we were sitting on the terrace discussing illogical fears.

All my life I have been terrified of spiders and I was explaining this to Roger, who at the time, was appearing in the highly successful TV Western series 'Maverick'.

Half way through my description of my eight-legged terror Roger quietly raised his hand. 'Mike, don't move. Just shut up and don't move. Stay absolutely still.'

I had no idea what was happening, but his normally smiling face looked sombre enough to be for real. Suddenly he leant forward and with a backward flip of his hand brushed the arm of the chair I was sitting in. As he began to move I noticed a small black spider on the arm.

Grown men shouldn't run away, but I leapt up and ran into the apartment, shaking with fright. Roger followed me, sat me down and explained: 'Sorry to scare you like that, but it was a black widow spider. There are lots in California and they can kill you.'

Roger later became the international star he is today as James Bond, but for none of his '007' exploits, even if they were reality, could match up to that day in Westwood.

Among British comics the man generally acknowledged as the greatest theatrical clown is Norman Wisdom. His was a talent I recognised when he was still a merchant seaman just after the end of World War Two.

Norman appeared at my office in Denmark Street (in those days London's 'Tin Pan Alley') and asked if I could get him work as a comedian. I admired his guts because he had never appeared on the professional stage in his life.

'What do you do?' I asked and he replied with a comic shadow boxing routine. I signed him to a ten per cent agency contract immediately and put him in a variety show at Clapham, South London.

That show went on tour for four weeks and then I produced a revue called 'New Names Make News', Norman was in it...as the star. A few months later I sold his contract for a few hundred pounds to a producer called Bert Montague. I did this because Bert told me, and rightly, that he could do bigger things for Norman than I could. I wasn't in Bert's league in those days and I felt it unfair to tie Norman down. I never made more than those few pounds from him but I did have the satisfaction of seeing my early faith in him justified.

My biggest mistake as potential star-spotter started off on the wrong foot – with a telephone call from Australia.

I was sound asleep at my home in Denham, Buckinghamshire late at night when the telephone rang. As I lifted it to my ear I was greeted with:

'Michael Sullivan? This is John Burls from Melbourne, Australia.'

The voice belonged to one of my closest Australian friends, a disc jockey whose interest in music was occasionally overshadowed by his fascination with the products of various distilleries. One night he paid so much attention to the latter that I had to take over his live spot from a Sydney night club, the Latin Quarter, and pretend to the listening millions that I was Burls with a bad case of laryngitis. Meantimes the real Mr Burls was fast asleep under the turntable deck.

John actually got away with it and we became, and remained, firm friends.

'John Burls, you old piss pot! How are you doing? Getting plenty?'

There was a polite cough from 13,000 miles. 'Michael Sullivan, we are on the air live...'

I cottoned on and said in a very different voice: 'John, dear boy. How splendid to hear you. Did I hear somebody else on the line?' Thus the sensitive broadcasting chiefs in strait-laced Melbourne were spared the difficulty of explaining away my profanity.

Burls replied: 'Michael I have already told our listeners who you are. We are running a contest to find a new girl singer. The first prize is a round trip to London. The object of this call is to ask if you would add to the prize by presenting the girl in cabaret in your wonderful city.'

I guaranteed the winner a fortnight's cabaret work at the Celebrité, a night club off Bond Street in London, wished

John a successful contest and hung up.

Instead of one girl a pair of very pretty Australians arrived in London. A double act had won the competition . . . and one of them was Olivia Newton-John!

These days she is one of the most successful girl recording artists in the world. Then, as I watched her perform she did not turn me on at all. In fact after the two weeks at the Celebrité when she told me that she and her partner wanted to stay and work in Britain I handed her over to my right-hand man Bill Roberton and for two years Bill booked Olivia and her friend on small-time dates around the country. They were a very 'saleable' act, but I could never see either of them as star material.

Which just goes to show how wrong you can be! I let one of the world's biggest pop names slip through my fingers. That, IS show business.

One young girl whose potential I recognised the first time I saw her on stage was Julie Andrews, now a multi-millionaire actress and singer.

I was the agent for Julie's parents, Ted and Barbara Andrews, a musical double act, and one evening Ted told me: 'We're going to bring our daughter Julie into the act. Can you get her on the billing?'

The billing the following week for the Grand Theatre, Doncaster read 'Ted and Barbara Andrews and introducing Julie Andrews.' Julie was only 15 at the time of this, her first professional engagement, but after seeing her and hearing her sing in that true, clear voice she still has today, I changed the billing for their next date at the King's Palace Theatre, Preston.

This time it read 'Julie Andrews with Ted and Barbara Andrews'. After one week in the business the girl was topping the bill!

Unkown to me Ted and Barbara had already signed Julie to an agent called Charles Tucker, an American, who had obviously told Barbara that he could open the doors across the Atlantic for Julie.

Barbara, a good professional herself, had recognised her

young daughter's talents and took Tucker's offer, knowing that he could do more for Julie than I could.

But I have always regretted that I didn't get the opportunity to try.

The 'search for a star' routine once turned full circle for me and I very nearly ended up on the other side of an agent's desk – paying the ten per cent instead of earning it.

But Adolf Hitler managed to put an end to that...

In July 1939 when I was in partnership with Charles Harvard we handled a skating act who were going to appear in an American film production. I had to take some pictures of them to a Paramount talent spotter at the film company's offices in London's Lower Regent Street.

The man I went to see was an American called Clovelly who had discovered stars such as Alan Ladd and Veronica Lake.

After dealing with our skaters his conversation took an unexpected turn:

'You're from a theatrical family? Ever acted?' he asked.

'No. I'm an agent.'

'You might try acting. It can pay better. Do you have any pictures of yourself?'

By now I was getting hooked. Could I really be a film star?

I promised I'd be at the office the following day with pictures of myself and a few weeks later, along with a crowd of other hopefuls I was screen-tested at Elstree Studios, a few miles out of London in the Hertfordshire countryside.

Among them was actor Richard Greene and we were among the lucky few who were offered a seven year contract with the studio. Mine was for £50 a week rising to £100 after two and a half years.

I floated home and waiting for the confirmation letter.

Days later Hitler marched on Poland and the letter never came.

But that's show business...

I concentrated on the agency business, then my glorious career in the Royal Air Force... and back to being an agent, but the fates must have been keeping an eye on me because in the late Nineteen Forties the call to act came again.

My business was in a deep depression. I had a staff of twelve and it took me all my time to find their wages, with enough over to provide me with a cheese roll for lunch.

But somehow I had managed to take a month's vacation in the South of France. I returned to London with a deep tan and my long hair bleached blond by the Mediterranean sun.

One of my acts that was still working was playing the London Palladium, as a support to the great Danny Kaye and one evening I went to the theatre. At the stage door a mob of Danny's fans were waiting on his arrival and as I stepped out of my taxi, wearing a very expensive camel hair overcoat, which all the best agents had in those days, one of the crowd shouted:

'There he is!'

I was pushed, shoved and clawed at and finally rescued by the doorman and a couple of stage hands.

My precious coat was in tatters, but the incident paid off.

After his season at the Palladium Danny Kaye was making a film at Shepperton Studios entitled 'The General' with Swedish star Mai Zetterling as his leading lady.

Late one afternoon I took a call from a casting agent asking me if I had anyone on my books who could stand in for Danny in the shots where he didn't have to be seen in close up and for the times when the lighting cameraman needed to line up his shots without using the star.

I told the casting man I had just the person. His name was Teddy Wightlaw and he would be at the Mikado Suite at the Savoy Hotel prompt at seven that evening.

Exactly on time Teddy Wightlaw, alias Michael Sullivan, was escorted to the suite by a hotel bell-boy.

I was invited into the room and the film's director looked me up and down and then introduced me to Mai Zetterling. I was told to sit next to her and then instructed:

'Turn left, turn right, hold Miss Zetterling with your back to me.

'You'll do.'

During all this Danny Kaye was at the other side of the room in deep discussion with his secretary. He never so much as acknowledged me – and I didn't get much change out of Mai Zetterling either.

But I got the job and I danced along the hotel corridors on the way out, humming to myself. I was getting thirty pounds a day as Danny's double, which was about three times as much as the agency was earning.

I even splashed out on a taxi to take me to the studio, convinced that this was the start of bigger and better things, a whole new career.

Until, after a few days shooting, the production manager asked me for my union card.

With that my film career came to an abrupt end and the next day Teddy Wightlaw was back behind the desk in Shaftesbury Avenue playing Michael Sullivan.

The true agent knows no limits, no fears, when it comes to promoting and building up a likely looking prospects into a star. The merest glimpse of a pot of gold on the horizon will push him to any lengths and make him take any risk with life, love, limb or money. His or yours.

Preferably yours.

Simon Oates is a moderately successful and very good-looking English actor. At one time I fixed a TV series for him and also managed to sign him for a couple of film parts. I had a lot of faith in the boy. He could act and he looked right – and then I saw him on the screen.

It was easy to spot what was wrong and how to put it right. I called Simon to my office and explained: 'It's like this, old lad: you have got to have a nose job.'

What he'd been born with had not done him much harm and he was, naturally, a little reluctant to face the surgeon's knife, but agents stay in business because of their persuasive powers and I was better than the next when it came to talking somebody into a deal.

Simon took his nose and my money to get the job done. I put up the £175 as an investment and because I have always believed in putting my money where somebody else's nose is.

As an example of cosmetic surgery it worked well, and although I am convinced that he looks all the better for that operation, Simon has never made it to the glittering top of his profession...

And I've never had my £175 back.

Business deals, even marriages, have been fixed over a game of golf and in show business this is the case more than in any other area.

Because all entertainment is founded upon theatre and because the theatre is an evening event people who work in it have more spare time on their hands during the days than anybody else.

This daylight leisure time makes golf an ideal game for 'pros'... you have only to watch the pro-am matches on your TV screen to realise that. If there is a 'game by appointment' to show business it is surely golf. It is my game and I am glad that I did not get involved with it before I took my early retirement and moved to Spain. If I had known about golf before that I would never have been in the office long enough to make the money to quit.

Marbella, my home in Southern Spain, is not only one of the most golf-crazy areas in the world, it also boasts (because of the golf, the sunshine and the relaxed style of living there) a vast number of show business personalities who have made the place their temporary or permanent home.

One of them is film star Sean Connery. He is there almost on a permanent basis. Another is comedian Eric Sykes who has a house in Marbella and spends a lot of his spare time there.

They both play golf... devotedly... and during one game in Spain, Sean recommended me to Eric as an agent. The comic had tax problems and although I was determined to stay out of the active side of the business I was persuaded to make a deal with Eric.

In three years I trebled his earnings and sorted out his worries with the tax man. I also learned a lot about the man.

Comedians are rarely what they seem on stage or on the screen and in this Eric runs true to form.

That hesitant, soft voiced, gawkish character he portrays hides an explosive temper. One of the worst I have ever encountered.

Golf brings out the best – and the worst – in the people who play and this is especially true in the case of Eric Sykes. If he misses a shot on the course his anger is rarely contained.

He can go absolutely white with rage and his behaviour can so easily spoil the game.

Off the course I have had my brushes with Eric and one of the most memorable was when he was working in a summer show with the late Hattie Jacques at the Winter Gardens Theatre in Blackpool.

I had arranged for Eric to star in a re-make of the comedy classic 'Charley's Aunt' for Yorkshire Television and he was also writing the script from the original play.

The script was late, very late, in arriving and Duncan Wood, head of the TV company's light entertainment division, was getting worried.

Together Duncan and I went to see Eric at the theatre. We waited until after the show before going to his dressing room... and we couldn't have picked a worse time.

The show had not been too well received by the audience that evening (you always get nights like that no matter how good the cast and the material are) and Eric was in a foul mood. When I tackled him over the script he blew his top:

'I didn't want to do it. I never wanted to do it. I only did it because you talked me into it,' he thundered at me.

'Let's get this straight', I countered – at the top of my voice in case he should later try to use his deafness as an excuse. 'You wanted to do the bloody thing. You asked me to fix it. You signed the contract. Now stop whining and get down to it. When you are a little more civilised call me at my hotel. Perhaps tomorrow'.

Having put Mr Sykes in his place I left and the following day he started work on the script again and eventually delivered it to Duncan's office.

Three years after I first took Eric on as a client and after three years of work during which time I had cleared up his financial problems and pushed his earnings way up I received a letter from him. I have forgotten the exact wording, but the last part of it went something like this:

'... you have taught me one thing, how to make money.'

That's gratitude for you. It's also show business.

What follows is a short aptitude test for any young man – or, for that matter, woman – wanting to make their way in the world:

You are invited to the home of one of the biggest international names in your field, a man whose earning power runs into millions of dollars each year. You are the friend of a guest and unknown to your host and all the other celebrities around his luxurious swimming pool.

You are invited to swim, have prepared for it by bringing your trunks with you, and take to the water.

Either the touch of the water or the sound of it lapping around acts as a 'trigger' and you desperately want to pee. Desperately.

You are far enough away from anybody to be able to take a chance. You do so and ... presto! The water around you turns mauve. It has been treated with a chemical that is used in many public swimming pools to embarrass the phantom piddlers.

The question is: How do you get out of that one?

If anyone knows the answer please send it to me (not more than fifty words on a postcard) because I've never been able to apologise to Dean Martin for what I did at his Hollywood home!

Until her tragic and untimely death in 1962 at the age of 36, Marilyn Monroe was the Hollywood sex symbol to beat them all. Even today, more than 20 years later, the mere mention of her name evokes sighs of appreciation from every man who has ever seen so much as a photograph of her and twinges of jealousy from their womenfolk.

Being confined to a bedroom alone with a naked and very sexy Marilyn must have been the idea of paradise for a billion men. Well, it happened to me and all I got out of it was the emnity of one of the most powerful men in the international film business.

I was in Hollywood with my fourth wife, Greek dancer Lily Berde (actually Lily was the only one of the five I never formally married, but when you live with someone for ten years the lack of a certificate and an entry in a register does not really matter too much) and we had met up with an old friend, Greek actor Nico Minardos.

Nico, a handsome young contract player with Twentieth Century Fox, had been doing passably well in his career... and a damn sight better in his love life.

His good looks and charm had always ensured plenty of success with the girls, but at this time he had really struck gold. Nico and Marilyn had become lovers.

Marilyn was a girl who spread her favours fairly widely and one who was also currently benefitting was Spyros Skouras, the ageing President of Twentieth Century Fox, her boss, Nico's boss, a Very Important Man indeed – and another Greek.

Nico and Marilyn had made every effort to keep their affair a secret, but Hollywood is just about the gabbiest town in the world and Spyros became suspicious.

One afternoon I was in my room at the Beverley Carlton hotel when I had an anguished call from Nico who was living about twenty yards away in one of the hotel's bungalows.

'I'm here with Marilyn and Skouras is on his way. We haven't got time to get rid of her. What do we do. Help me!'

Nico, I later learned had had a call while in bed from another Greek, Nicky, who worked in the Canteen at Twentieth Century Fox, warning him of Skouras's arrival, but not warning him in time.

This whole business was rapidly becoming a full-scale Greek drama!

Years of cheating on my wives and having to cover up for it had developed in me a sixth sense for moments like this.

'Get your pants on and get into my room quickly,' I told him. 'I'm already dressed and while you're doing that I'll call the reception desk and tell them you've switched rooms. When Skouras comes looking for you he'll find you alone and he wouldn't dream of checking every room in the place for her.'

I replaced the telephone then rang the reception desk telling them that Nico had changed with me and to direct any visitors for him to my old room. Then I dashed across to Nico's little love nest, passing him on the way.

In the bungalow the exquisite – and rather ruffled – Miss Monroe was sitting in bed with the sheets held up to her chin, modestly covering that exceptional body. I introduced myself hurriedly and told her of the plan, then sat coyly on a chair in a corner.

We didn't talk, just sat looking at each other and hoping it would work.

It didn't. Minutes later the door crashed opened and Skouras strode in. The expressions on his face ran through anger, surprise and then confusion. He had found what he had been told he would find (and secretly hoped he wouldn't) but the wrong man was in the trap.

It took a second or two for him to turn from me to Marilyn.

'Where's Nico?' he bellowed at her.

'Nico? Nico who?' (in her best little girl bemused voice).

'Marilyn I don't want to argue now. Just come with me. And who is this man?'

'He is a great friend of Lily Berde,' she replied and Skouras's face registered some recognition. After all, he had seen Lily dancing in a Paris cabaret, asked to meet her and invited her to work in Hollywood.

'We'll see about that later,' he said. 'You (pointing at me) get out!'

I was in enough unwarranted trouble already and wasn't in any mood to argue or explain. I got.

Later Nico and I learned that our room switch had not been notified to everyone on the reception desk. There had not been time. When Skouras arrived and asked for Nico's room number he spoke to one man who had not been told.

Nico continued to see – and make love to – Marilyn for a while and Skouras never really confirmed his suspicions about their affair, but his Greek anger had to be assuaged in some way and it was.

For doing nothing more than helping a pal out of a jam I was banned from the Fox studios ... and Lily along with me.

If there's a moral to this it must be:

When Greek and Greek go for the same girl – stay out of the bloody way!

When he wasn't singing and recording some of the most popular songs the world has ever known Harry Lillis Crosby seemed to be playing golf. The game was such a passion with Bing, the 'Old Groaner' that the public image of him will always be a man with a light-weight trilby raked on the side of his head, a pipe in his mouth, gently swinging a golf club.

It was my delight and privilege to play with Bing during the last year of his life; to win a bet that was paid off in the form of a wonderful birthday surprise for my wife Dany and discuss with him a deal that, regrettably, never came off.

My home in Spain is literally on the El Paraiso golf course just outside Marbella. A short distance from it is another course, the Aloha, and it was here that an American friend, Bill Richmond, introduced me to Bing.

Bill, a terrific golfer who plays off a five handicap and often appeared in Bing's golfing classics, had returned to Spain and was setting up a four ball game on the Aloha course.

He invited another friend, Pat Ryan, who runs a bar in Marbella, and I to take part. The fourth member of the quartet was Mr Crosby.

Bing, at that stage in his life, was not the superb golfer many people thought he was. But for a man in his seventies he showed all the style of someone who had once been very, very good.

He played off a handicap of twelve and although his age had obviously cut down on the strength and power of his drives he was an excellent pitcher and putter. He was also, as you would imagine, the most relaxed golfer I have ever seen.

True to all of my dreams of him, he hummed and sang to himself while walking the course; let nothing upset him and was the perfect companion for a game in the sun.

The game was both enjoyable and memorable because of

his presence and – as golfers do – we struck a few side bets on the way around those eighteen holes. One of them, between Bing and I, carried no stakes. It was just one of those 'I'll bet you that...' wagers and I won.

'You've won. How do you want paying?' he asked.

'If you don't mind, it will cost you a song,' I replied. 'It's my wife's birthday and we're having a party for her at my home – it's very near here. When we've finished I'd like to invite you along. And would you sing "Happy Birthday" to her?'

Later that day, around the pool at my house, Dany cut her birthday cake while the man who had sung to the world for more than forty years crooned to her alone.

When agent and artist get together it's only natural that the talk should turn to business. On the golf course I gently tackled Bing about his future plans and told him how much I would like to present him in a series of British Concerts.

The plan was to present him with Bruce Forsyth in a 'Bing and Bruce' show with Bruce appearing for the first half and Bing the second. I explained that Bruce did a similar sort of an act to the one done by Sammy Davis in the United States – a bit of everything – and that his popularity in Britain was very high.

Bing replied that he had heard of Bruce, but never seen him. He liked the idea and we arranged to meet later in the year in New York to hammer out a deal.

I eventually went to New York where I saw Bing appear. Supporting him on the bill was an English comic, Ted Rogers. When I went back stage after the show I was told that Bing was tied up, but that he had expected me. Would I leave my telephone number and he would contact me in the morning.

I did this and then called in on Ted. I had been so impressed with his act that I promised him that if I could ever find the right vehicle for him in Britain I would be in touch. That opportunity, for both of us, did occur with 'Three-Two-One', the TV game that has made him a star, but the story of that comes later.

In the morning I received a call inviting me to lunch at New York's Gaslight Room with Bing. There, among the old prints and dark leather furniture we were served our roast beef by leggy, busty waitresses wearing fishnet tights. They hardly seemed to fit in the with the image of an English gentlemen's club which the place tried to achieve.

Over that lunch Bing and I hammered out the basis of a deal on the tour. So far I hadn't signed Bruce Forsyth but I was sure that he would jump at the chance of sharing top-billing with Bing Crosby. The concerts would be held in six British centres. Leeds, Birmingham, Brighton, Glasgow and London and one still to be decided but most probably Manchester. For his participation Bing would receive a massive sixty per cent of the gross taking PLUS air fares and hotels paid for himself and his entourage.

If that sounds as though I stood to make very little money I should explain that I planned to 'price the house' so that the average cost of a ticket would be £40.

That way there would be plenty of cash in it for everybody.

'I am only doing this for the money,' said Bing. 'It sounds like it should be an easy tour. That and the money are the attractions for me.'

Strange that a man with so much should – at his age – still want to earn more, but I wasn't prepared to question his motives ... just earn along with him.

'I want your office to draw up the contracts so that there can be no question of arguments over the deal,' I said. He agreed, we finished our lunch and when I left New York for Spain I was convinced I had one of the greatest concert tours of all time in my pocket.

Deals like these take months, and often longer, to set up. I was prepared to wait, knowing that it could be a long time before we got the tour under way.

All of my hopes crashed one day in October 1977 when I picked up a Spanish newspaper. All I could understand from one of the headlines was 'Bing Crosby Dead'.

He had dropped dead while playing a game of golf in Madrid and that was the end of my concert tour with him.

There is no good way of dying but I am sure that if Bing could have picked the circumstances of his death he would have chosen to go in just the way he did.

In the morning I received a call inviting me to lunch at New York's Gaslight Room with Bing. There, among the old prints and dark leather furniture we were served our roast beef by leggy, busty waitresses wearing fishnet tights. They hardly seemed to fit in the with the image of an English gentlemen's club which the place tried to achieve.

Over that lunch Bing and I hammered out the basis of a deal on the tour. So far I hadn't signed Bruce Forsyth but I was sure that he would jump at the chance of sharing top-billing with Bing Crosby. The concerts would be held in six British centres. Leeds, Birmingham, Brighton, Glasgow and London and one still to be decided but most probably Manchester. For his participation Bing would receive a massive sixty per cent of the gross taking PLUS air fares and hotels paid for himself and his entourage.

If that sounds as though I stood to make very little money I should explain that I planned to 'price the house' so that the average cost of a ticket would be £40.

That way there would be plenty of cash in it for everybody.

'I am only doing this for the money,' said Bing. 'It sounds like it should be an easy tour. That and the money are the attractions for me.'

Strange that a man with so much should – at his age – still want to earn more, but I wasn't prepared to question his motives... just earn along with him.

'I want your office to draw up the contracts so that there can be no question of arguments over the deal,' I said. He agreed, we finished our lunch and when I left New York for Spain I was convinced I had one of the greatest concert tours of all time in my pocket.

Deals like these take months, and often longer, to set up. I was prepared to wait, knowing that it could be a long time before we got the tour under way.

All of my hopes crashed one day in October 1977 when I picked up a Spanish newspaper. All I could understand from one of the headlines was 'Bing Crosby Dead'.

He had dropped dead while playing a game of golf in Madrid and that was the end of my concert tour with him.

There is no good way of dying but I am sure that if Bing could have picked the circumstances of his death he would have chosen to go in just the way he did.

Scene Four: The Stars and Their Lovers

Bruce Forsyth has always dreamed of repeating in the United States the phenomenal success he has had in Britain. Whether he has or not depends very much upon whom you listen to: Bruce or some of the critics.

I may not have been able to guarantee Bruce any lasting fame and popularity there but I did manage to ensure that he would play to a full house for one date I was setting up in New York.

And I called in the Mafia to help!

Shortly after Sidney James died I had lunch with Bruce in the 21 Room in Mayfair, London. I had a commitment with Thames Television for Sid to appear in a play for them and I wanted Bruce to do me a favour and take over the part, which he did.

Over the lunch I mentioned to Bruce that I was seeing Bernard Delfont, one of the most powerful men in British and world entertainment that afternoon. I had been a director of Bernie's agency and still had close ties with him.

'If you're seeing him could you do me a favour?' asked Bruce. 'I have done so many things like charity shows for him and he has always promised that if the chance ever came up he would "break" me in the States. Just remind him and see if there's anything he can fix.'

At my meeting with Bernard Delfont I spoke of Bruce and his American dream.

'If you can show me that he could mean anything there I'll do my best for him. In fact, why don't you go over and see if we can set something up?' said Bernie.

I was already retired and living in Spain. I had nothing else much to do, so with Bernie offering to pay my expenses for the trip I flew to the U.S.

Believing that with the maximum television exposure before a New York opening night I could grab the interest of American public in Bruce, I went first to Los Angeles. There, with a lot of help from Bernard Delfont's brother Lord (Lew) Grade, I arranged for Bruce to appear on the Johnny Carson show, one of the nation's most important chat shows.

Former singer Dinah Shore's daily TV shows were also on my 'shopping list' and once again I went in through the back door to get Bruce on one of them. Dinah's close friend is Mrs Anne Douglas, wife of actor Kirk, and my wife Dany knew Kirk and Anne as old friends from her movie-making days which were not that far in the past. Through Anne the Dinah Shore programme was arranged for Bruce.

From glittering Las Vegas came the Merv Griffin chat show and again... the old pal's act came into play.

I had dinner with singer Dick Haymes and told him: 'Rich, I need the Griffin show'.

'They've been asking me to do it for months,' said Haymes, 'but I don't fancy the drag to Las Vegas. But for you I'll do it if they guarantee to put your boy on.'

Dick called the show's booker and a few days later I went with him to Las Vegas where he appeared on the programme. The Griffin people said they would keep their end of the bargain. Bruce was in.

My next attempt to get Bruce on American TV proved that in this world without friends and contacts you're nowhere. I got a flat refusal from a station in Philadelphia to use him, but with three of the biggest chat shows in the country in my pocket I felt confident enough to fly to New York and make a provisional booking on the 3,800 seat Lincoln Centre.

Then I called in on the William Morris Agency, one of

America's most important, to see old friends and tell them of my plans.

The reactions numbed me. Summed up they amounted to: 'Michael, you have got to be out of your mind. He doesn't mean a thing here and even with those chat shows he will die. You won't sell a ticket for the place.'

I felt all alone in the world. I had been so sure that all I needed was the right amount of TV exposure to pack the Lincoln Centre that I had forgotten I was working in foreign territory. Maybe they were right, those friends at William Morris.

There still had to be a trump or two I could use, somebody I could go to for help. The business with Bruce had now become such a challenge that I was determined to win somehow.

In the theatre the system of handing out free tickets like confetti for a show that is not doing well in order to make it look like a success is known as 'papering the house'. That was what I needed to do with Bruce at the Lincoln Centre. But how?

Mentally I ran through a list of all the people and organisations I could have turned to in London and tried to match them with their American equivalents. It did not work.

'Jesus, it looks as though I'll need the Mafia to persuade anybody to buy a ticket,' I said to myself.

The Mafia! I had found the answer, at least part of it. All I needed now was the method to contact the right people.

When you have four ex-wives it is impossible to stay angry with any one of them for too long. It is far too exhausting and emotionally tiring and for that reason I have always been on good terms with my 'exes', particularly Number Three, Juhni.

After we divorced Juhni married a man called Bob Dicks and we, too, became friendly. Bob used to run casinos in Havana, Cuba. Gambling and The Mob have always gone together. In desperation I telephoned Bob at his home in London.

I explained my problems and he told me: 'Mike, stay by your phone for an hour or two. There's somebody I need to call. I'll come back to you.'

When Bob's call did come he gave me a number in Philadelphia and told me to call it: 'The Don is waiting to hear from you.'

Scenes from 'The Godfather' (all of them the bloody ones) raced through my mind, but I made the call and was told courteously from the other end: 'Mr Sullivan, my man will be in New York tomorrow. He will have lunch with you.'

He did, too. A polite, business-like guy who told me: 'the Lincoln Centre will be full on the night you want it. Just give me the date and it will be full and they will pay.'

It all sounded too incredible. 'How can you guarantee that? Just tell me. How can you?' I asked.

'We *own* the Teamsters, Mr Sullivan. They will do as they are told.' The Teamsters are America's transport union and their links with the underworld have been a matter of concern to the American government for decades.

His confidence was contagious, so I decided to push my luck and by the time we parted he had also promised that Bruce would be on that Philadelphia TV show which had earlier turned him down.

In return for all this I had to do – and pay – nothing. The old pal's act works even with the Mafia.

I had done it! I had filled the house with The Mob! I flew back to London to buy Bob Dicks and Juhni the finest dinner in town and to break the news to Bruce and Bernard Delfont.

I kept the dinner date, but there was news waiting for me when I got back. In my absence Bruce had signed a contract with another agent and all my work went out of the window. All I could do now was telephone and make my apologies to all the people whose friendship I had used.

Bruce subsequently went to the United States and appeared there, but he got nothing like the reception he would have had from the Mafia's hand-picked audience.

In an odd way perhaps fate was paying me back for a gag I had pulled on Bruce a few years earlier when I was handling a variety tour. At one town the show visited, Bruce was appearing at a nearby theatre and – as show business people do – we met for drinks after work.

Bruce had, at that time, parted from his first wife Penny. He has always fancied himself as a ladies' man and I had found just the girl for him.

Girl? Well, that was not strictly true.

In my show we had an outstanding 'drag' artist called Terri Durham, a female impersonator who had looks that most women would like to have.

Terri even had the figure to go with them. He had had silicone bust 'improvement' and unless you got VERY close to him you were convinced that he was a beautiful girl.

I did some surreptitious checking to find out that Terri and Bruce had never met each other and that Bruce had never heard of our sexy looking 'girl'. Then I invited Terri to drinks after the show after telling him of my plan.

I got to work on Bruce, raving over this fantastic looking girl we had in the show and how much she wanted to meet him. 'You could be on to a live 'un here, Bruce. Play your cards right and it will be no problem'.

With two or three other friends, Bruce and I were drinking happily in my hotel suite.

'Where is she? Where's this lovely bird you've found for me? I haven't got all night, you know,' said Bruce.

'Patience, patience, she'll be along,' I said, although by now it had got so late that I was beginning to fear that Terri had ducked out of her date.

The evening had reached the stage when I thought Bruce had waited long enough and would get up and leave when the door opened and, to my relief, 'Miss' Durham made her entrance. He looked stunning and Bruce was more than suitably impressed.

The rest of us – who all knew Terri – made sure she would be driven to Bruce by behaving as badly as we could towards him.

'They are so crude, aren't they?' said the charming Mr Forsyth. 'Why don't you come and sit with me, my dear.'

While the rest of us carried on with our drinking and talking, ignoring the couple in the corner, sitting 'with' Bruce had developed a little and Terri was on his lap. The chivalrous Bruce had not only saved the lady from our vulgarity... it was perfectly obvious by now that he was saving her all for himself.

Bruce's gentlemanly behaviour had turned to affection and the affection was now becoming hot-blooded.

Passion may have its blind moments, but everyone has to come up for air some time. It was then that the awful realization hit Bruce.

He looked around the room, his eyes wide open and that long jaw getting dangerously near to hitting the floor.

'Here! It's... it's a feller!'

He dumped Terri on the floor and headed for the door. He was shaking as he pulled it open and made off along the hallway, while from the doorway the rest of us called:

'Dirty old man! Trying to take advantage of a young girl – you ought to be ashamed. Just because you're a big name you think you can get away with anything.'

Other guests in the hotel were opening their doors to find out what was happening in the early hours of the morning.

But this was one occasion when Bruce Forsyth wanted to stay well out of the public eye.

Through the smoky haze of a London night club at two in the morning the striking looking woman sitting alone at a nearby table looked very familiar, but I could not fit a name to the face. To get a closer look at her I made an unnecessary trip to the men's room, passing her table as I went.

As I did I recognised her as Hollywood actress Ava Gardner, once voted the most beautiful woman in the world and the star of some of the most successful films of the Forties and Fifties. She was, I thought, obviously waiting to be joined by her escort for the evening... lucky man!

In those days of the mid-Fifties I was running the TV department of impresario Jack Hylton's business and one of my jobs was finding and booking acts for the Friday night TV show 'Albany Club'. This meant that I spent most of my nights in clubs, and the Stork Room, in London's Swallow Street was a regular spot on my list. It was here that I had seen Ava Gardner.

A few nights later I was in the Stork again. She too was there and, as before, she was alone at a table.

In the weeks that followed it seemed that every time I walked into the Stork, Ava was there – and always alone. I never stayed until closing time so could only guess that she was waiting for somebody.

'She's always in here,' I said to 'Pip' Mariello, the club's head waiter one morning.

'What does she do? She always seems to be alone.'

'Maybe she's waiting for the right man,' explained the world-weary 'Pip' with a shrug.

Why any woman looking like that – and at the time she was in her early thirties and truly magnificent – would be without a man was beyond me, and one night when I was drinking in the Stork with a Channel Island theatre owner called Sydney James I repeated what 'Pip' had told me, adding:

'Maybe you've got a chance, Sydney. Go and chat her up. See how you get on.'

Sydney spent the rest of his time in the club charming the lady. And this time I was the one sitting alone. When I left for home they were still together. I am too much of a gentlemen to have asked what did happen later, but he smiled a lot when he saw me again.

Over the years I saw Ava occasionally in London but we never met each other and I was saddened by the gradual deterioration of that beautiful face.

About fifteen years after I had first seen her in the Stork Room an old friend in the theatre business, a woman called 'Bumble Dawson', telephoned me. 'Bumble' had been looking after Ava and she was worried about her and asked if Dany, my wife, and I would invite her to dinner 'so that she can meet some other people.'

I arranged a dinner party and invited singer Dick Haymes to it. Dick was also an American, he had appeared in 'One Touch Of Venus' with Ava. And he was off the booze. They would have plenty in common to talk about and he wouldn't lead her astray.

I had sent my car from my home in Esher, Surrey, to London to pick Ava up. She entered the house, was introduced to Dany and greeted Dick as an old Hollywood colleague.

She had very little to say and as soon as she had finished her first course she stood up and announced: 'I don't want any more to eat. I would like another drink and I would like to lie down before the fire.'

Like any good host, I gave way to my guest, escorted her to a settee in front of a log fire, poured her a drink and went back to my dinner.

Dany, Dick and I got so involved in our conversation that we forgot all about our sleeping beauty... until we left the dinner table.

There was no Ava on the settee and after waiting for half an hour in case she had crept off to the bathroom we realised that she had disappeared. I called George Pirie my chauffeur and while Dany searched the house, he, Dick and I looked around the grounds.

No Ava.

George Pirie took my Rolls Royce and drove towards the centre of Esher while I got into Dany's small car and headed in the other direction, towards Cobham.

After a few hundred yards I found Ava Gardner alone on an unlit country road, a menace to herself and any traffic that was using it. I stopped, got her into the car easily enough and took her back to the house.

We waited until an unsuccessful George appeared, handed her over to him and he drove her back to London.

During the entire period – from her disappearance to

my returning her to my house – Ava did not utter one word.

We have never met since.

That old fairy tale of the Prince and the show girl came true when lovely Dawn Addams, a young British actress married the Italian Prince Vittorio Massimo in 1954.

It was one of those marriages fated not to last and when Dawn eventually left her prince she returned to London, with no money... just a very beautiful diamond necklace to show for her years among the Roman aristocracy.

I became her agent for a while but work was hard to find in an ailing film business and Dawn – at this time living with comedian Michael Howard who had plenty of problems of his own – was flat broke.

She took the necklace along to her bank manager and asked him for a five thousand pound overdraft against it and offered to leave it with him as security. The jewellery was worth far more than the overdraft and he agreed.

Two weeks later Dawn needed money again and this time she had nothing left to sell or pledge so she pulled off a nifty little stroke.

Looking very chic and glamourous she called on the bank manager and asked him if she could please borrow her necklace for a couple of days. 'I have a big event to go to. It could mean lots of work and I want to look my best,' she purred.

The man couldn't resist her and like a father handing extra pocket money to a repentant schoolgirl he gave her the necklace, making her promise it would be back in his safe-keeping within three days.

Dawn's next call was on a manufacturing jeweler where she ordered an almost worthless 'paste' replica of the necklace to be made in a hurry. She got it within her three day time limit and dutifully took it to the bank.

The real necklace was then sold for something approaching its not inconsiderable real value.

And until Dawn paid off her overdraft the bank manager held on to the piece of junk, fully convinced that the five thousand was safe – secured by a bauble that wasn't worth one per cent of the value of the real item.

Dawn is now married to a retired British businessman, James White and lives in Malta, but at the time I was her agent she was going through a four-year long very stormy romance with Michael Howard.

The rows they had were very frequent and very temperamental. They often culminated with Michael threatening to commit suicide and I had suffered so many telephone calls from Dawn during those moments that I developed a thick, callous hide towards it all.

After being wakened late one night at my home by Dawn telling me: 'Mike, he's got a gun. He's pointing it at his head and he's going to pull the trigger. What shall I do?'

'Tell him to do it and then call me in the morning,' I said – and hung up.

I got the call the next day – from a very much alive Michael demanding to know how I could have been so brutal and upset Dawn so much.

And not one word about the gun...

From the time I was old enough to go to the 'tuppenny rush' at a Saturday morning cinema show I have been addicted to films and film-making. Movies have supplied my childhood fantasies and, in my adult years, a lot of eating and drinking money and today I still remain faithful to the heroes and heroines I met from a seat in the stalls.

One of the most enduring of all Hollywood stars was the late Humphrey Bogart who made the portrayal of cynical tough guys an art form.

He was, and is, a favourite of millions – me included. I had always wanted to meet the man and when I did it was hardly in the way I had thought it would be.

On second thoughts our introduction was in typical screen Bogart style... with a slap in the mouth!

I was in Hollywood in 1955 and was visiting the Paramount studios where Bogey was making one of his last films 'The Desperate Hours'. After watching some filming I was taken to the studio canteen and while eating lunch there I saw

Bogart come through the doors. He looked around the place, stopped and then started to walk again. This time he was coming in my direction and when he drew level he grabbed me by the shoulder and back-handed me across the face.

Even as he did it it was clear to see that he knew he had made a mistake.

'Je-sus! I'm sorry. Really sorry. You're not the guy. Please let me tell you this is all a mistake,' he said.

He never explained why he had been angry or who he was mad at, but he offered to make amends by entertaining me to dinner.

I dined with Bogart that evening at the Brown Derby, one of Hollywood's classiest and most star-studded restaurants. It was a pleasant uneventful evening and our conversation never seemed to touch on anything memorable, but for me just being with the man was an experience I would happily have taken a belting for any day.

He also arranged for me to be his guest at a Friars Club dinner that was given in his honour in New York and that evening has stayed in my memory because of one young comedian.

It was a strictly stag night and half the comedy world of America seemed to be there... all of them eager to get up with a funny routine.

This young man's act went something like this:

'Mr Bogart, when I was a kid I used to save up my dimes and nickels to go and see your films. Do you remember the war movie when you played a top sergeant?'

'Yep,' Bogey retorted.

'And you landed on a Jap held island with your troop?'
'Yep'.

'And your guys pushed the Japs back off the beach?'
'Yep'.

'And you finally took the airfield?'
'Yep'.

'And you personally ran with the flag and planted it in the ground.'

'Yep'.

'You fuckin' liar – it was John Wayne!'

One old-time Hollywood name I cannot recall with the affection I have for Bogart is Mischa Auer. Remember him? The lanky Russian who specialised in noble idiot parts and never stopped popping up in films for close on fifty years.

Shortly after World War Two the British public were so hungry for entertainment that any Hollywood name could cross the Atlantic and play to packed houses. Even Mickey Rooney did it. It was that easy.

But there is the exception in every business, and I got it... Mischa.

Leslie Grade, without doubt the greatest agent that ever worked in Britain, had been landed with him in a 'package' of American entertainers and having found the bad apple in his barrel he decided to sell him off to other bookers.

I paid him one thousand pounds (a fortune in those days) for one week at the Empire Theatre in Croydon. I would have had more fun using the money to light cigarettes with.

For a start the man had no act... nothing... and to top it all he was an absolute lush. He was drunk on stage and off and made no attempt to entertain anybody. The audiences started to walk out on the Monday evening, and unlike my five-legged sheep stunt they felt they had been taken and they DID tell their friends. Result: Nobody with ears came for the rest of the week.

Leslie and I fought over that deal for months, but finally in the interests of friendship and business harmony (and I suspect a mutual loathing for the biggest 'turkey' we had ever seen) he split the difference of my financial loss with me.

Entertainers – whatever they are: actors, singers, dancers, comics, even lion-tamers and fire-eaters – are not like ordinary people. If they were they would not be wearing another character's clothes, singing or speaking somebody else's lines and adopting different personalities for a living.

Their public and private images are nearly always totally different. Some of them are so easy to get along with that working for them as an agent or manager is a pleasure.

But when they are difficult they can make your life a living hell with tantrums and outsized egos.

I have had my share of both types and generally I have managed to cope. But Kathy Kirby was different.

That glossy-lipped, blonde singer who showed such promise in the Sixties just wasn't worth the trouble she brought me.

In 1963 I was approached by Ian Grant, a song-writer whom I had known for years. He had been sent to me by Bert Ambrose who, in his day, had been the most successful bandleader in Britain.

While playing at a dance hall in Ilford, Essex, Bert had heard a local girl sing. He was impressed and immediately took her under his wing. He managed and moulded her into a professional singer, but their relationship was far too close for two people with their explosive temperaments to get along professionally.

Ian took me to see Kathy singing at a private party in a London night club, the Jack of Clubs. Bert was there and we discussed how I could best handle Kathy.

I thought the girl had great potential and I signed a management deal with her. I routined a special act for her, booked dates and got her a recording contract with the Decca company.

But as I got to know her and Bert better I began to wish I had never got involved. Bert was continually interfering with my plans for her and the two of them would use me – and anybody else who happened to be around – as a 'sounding board' in the bitter rows they seemed to have daily. These embarrassingly unpleasant scenes would be sparked off by the most innocuous remark and could take place anywhere.

Our parting came just as Kathy was on the way to her biggest success as a recording star. In August 1963 she had entered the charts with 'Dance On'. The record reached eleventh place in the charts and stayed among the best sellers for 13 weeks.

With a start like that the follow-up record would be the most important of her career and for it we chose 'Secret Love'. It was released shortly before Christmas that year and I arranged three TV appearances for Kathy to plug the song. But for her to do them I had to get her out of an engagement in Norwich. I did this with the oldest white lie in the world: I told the bookers that she had not been well and needed some medical treatment. That cleared the way for the TV spots and I was prepared to deal with any comebacks later.

Those TV appearances were vital to the promotion of 'Secret Love', but when Kathy and Bert read of her 'sickness' they turned on me.

With a belief in her clean, virtually virginal image that bordered on the neurotic, Kathy told me: 'It sounds as though I have had an abortion. How dare you do this to me?'

Bert, over-protective as ever, weighed in and I walked out.

'Secret Love' eventually went to Number Four in the charts and was the biggest record Kathy ever made. Her career at the top lasted another two years and the last I heard of her was that, with Bert dead she was no longer singing.

Had it not been for the extraordinary relationship with Bert Ambrose she could, I am sure, still be a top-drawer performer, but the chemistry between them was wrong.

Few other television shows have been as popular with the British public as 'Sunday Night At The London Palladium'. With its straightforward variety formula it became a national institution and the launching pad for some very successful show business careers.

Every Sunday the show would sign off with all of the acts standing on the revolving stage, waving inanely to the millions watching at home.

That revolving stage never failed to close the show – until Dave King appeared on the programme.

Dave was a comic and singer before he became the excellent actor he is today. He was also a man with a reputation for being difficult. And he was my client.

I first saw Dave in a theatre production of 'A Funny Thing Happened On The Way To The Forum' and decided he had the talent to become a star performer. But I reckoned without his temperament. Dave knew he was good... and nobody could tell him anything.

He had upset a few people in the business and getting any publicity for him was not easy because of the enemies he had made among journalists.

After a lot of pushing and persuasion I got him a booking on the Palladium show. It was the biggest show case for talent in Britain and I knew his act was good enough to carry him to better things once enough people had seen him.

The trouble started at the rehearsal for the big show. Dave had been allocated a seven-minute 'spot' on it and stayed on stage for much longer. The producer spoke to me and I told Dave to cut his act down.

Mistakenly, I thought he had taken notice, but when the programme was broadcast live he stayed on for a full thirteen minutes. It's hard enough to get a comic off the stage if he is running over time in a theatre. On a live TV show it is impossible.

Dave threw the timing of the entire production out of gear and for the first and only time the show finished without the mass farewell from that revolving stage.

The producer was furious and Val Parnell, the TV boss who presented 'SNATLP' was apopleptic.

'Why, Dave? Why did you have to do it?' I asked.

'I was out there and they were enjoying it. Why should I cut it short?'

'You were ruining a show, there were other acts to consider...' I realised there was no point in arguing with the man. For the sake of just six minutes, he had thrown away his greatest chance.

Dave has only in recent years started to emerge as an actor of some considerable talent after a long time out of the public eye. I can only hope that he has grown up enough not to throw away any more golden opportunities.

When things go wrong in the lives of entertainers they rarely turn to their loved ones or their friends for advice and consolation. Instead they take their problems to the people who guide their *professional* lives... their agents and managers, believing, no doubt, that for the ten per cent it's all part of the service.

Agents spend as much time keeping their acts on a firm emotional footing as they do in getting work for them, but when Bill Owen came to me with his troubles I decided I needed some extra, expert help and called in Dick Emery.

Bill was appearing in the TV series 'Taxi!' with another of my clients, Sidney James, and he had fallen in love. For years he had been apparently happily married. Leaving his wife for another woman had been a tremendous wrench for him and he was having second thoughts.

'Mike,' he said when he telephoned me, 'I need some help, somebody to talk to. It's about this marriage business.'

I arranged to meet Bill, who has achieved the stardom he has always deserved in 'Last Of The Summer Wine', for lunch... and then called Emery.

Between us Dick and I had been married seven (or was it eight?) times and this was obviously a job for the professionals.

'Dear boy,' said Dick, when the three of us were seated around a table in a London restaurant. 'You have come to the right people. Michael and I are past masters in this business of divorce.' At the time Dick himself was in the middle of an affair with dancer Josephine Blake while still married to his third wife Vicki, but the aplomb with which he addressed poor, worried Bill disguised all that.

'Dick's right,' I chimed in. 'You have already left Edith and now you are suffering from a touch of the seconds. Don't. Calm down and think about it, because the awful thing about marriage is that you tend to remember only the good times and not the bad ones.

'But people like us... we have managed to reverse that philosophy. We remember the bad times.' Like a hypnotist pressing home a point into the sub-conscious I went on: 'Just think of the bad times, Bill... the bad times.

'Think of your marriage as a book that you have finished. Close the book and pick up another one, a new one.'

Then we had another drink.

Sullivan and Emery, marriage and divorce counsellors, did their work well. Bill never went back to his wife.

Dick and I did, but we were already on the final chapters of our own particular books.

Scene Five: Publicity Stunts

I had never seen a professional football match in my life, but I have been responsible for the greatest film about the game ever made – and I did it on a shoe-string.

The film is 'Goal' the 106-minute story of the 1966 World Cup and – come to think of it – I had never made a film either until then.

'Goal!' started shortly before the World Cup matches in 1966 when, at scriptwriter Leigh Vance's house I met a man called Octavio Senoret.

He said he was in films, I said I was in show business and for a while we talked about our mutual interests, but there was never any mention of making a movie together.

The following day Octavio telephoned me and told me that he was making a film of the World Cup but his French backer, who owned the rights, had dropped out. Would I be interested? I made a date with him that afternoon and went to see Leslie Grade, one of the three famous Grade Brothers, who I knew to be a great soccer fan and a director of a London team.

Leslie knew a lot about football and when I outlined the deal with him he said: 'O.K. Mike, go ahead with it. I'll get the money.'

I was so impressed with his enthusiasm that when I met Octavio I told him I would take the deal. Two days later his backer flew from Paris and Octavio bought the rights to film the World Cup from him.

Then the headaches began. Leslie Grade, who was managing director of London Management, the agency of which I was a director, told me he could not raise the cash for the film because of the risks involved.

I did not understand him until he explained that if a small, unknown country like Paraguay won the contest the film would be worthless. 'You will only know which territories you can sell it in once the final has been played,' he said.

The trouble was that I had committed myself to pay that Frenchman for the rights and the money had to come from somewhere. Payment was not due until after the film had been made, so the smartest thing to do seemed to be to get on and make it.

But how?

With Octavio I went to Samuelsons, the movie equipment and facilities company in London and set a deal with Michael Samuelson for them to provide the crew and the equipment. Octavio, who cheered me up immensely by letting me know that he, too, had never been involved in film production before, visited all the locations while I found a director, scriptwriter and narrator.

On the day we started shooting the arrival of teams at London's Heathrow Airport I had just seven hundred and fifty pounds towards the one hundred and eighteen thousand I needed to complete 'Goal!'

Octavio stayed in England while I flew around the world, selling off the film territory by territory to distributors. I pulled in about sixty thousand pounds from Greece, Hong Kong, Turkey, Japan and Singapore... but nobody in Britain was interested.

To keep the film going I invested five thousand pounds of my own money into it and talked Dick Emery into doing the same.

But on the evening before England met West Germany in the 1966 World Cup Final at Wembley everything fell apart. Michael Samuelson's crew downed tools. Michael had not been paid for their work and he had ordered them to stop.

There was only one thing to do. Talk.

Throughout the night Michael Samuelson, my lawyer Michael Simpkins and I sat in a hotel room arguing and getting no nearer finishing the film. It was then that I decided on my last, desperate throw:

'There's no point in talking any more,' I said to Michael Samuelson. 'There is only one solution. You have got to put up some money.'

Samuelson was not amused. 'I don't see how you can say...'

'Well,' I said. 'It goes like this: If you don't put some money in your men don't get paid – at least they don't get paid by me and then it's your problem. If they don't get paid they don't work and we have no film. If we have no film you don't get any money. And I have nothing.'

He put up fifteen thousand pounds.

The next day, when the final was played I went to the cinema. Even with all that I had at stake I still could not raise any interest in soccer.

I left the cinema to be told that England had beaten West Germany. My worries were over!

Once again I was wrong. Still no distributor in Britain was interested in my film. I managed to sell it in France, but I desperately needed a major company to take the film for showing in Britain and North America.

To get away from it all I took my wife Lily back to her homeland Greece for a short holiday. That trip was in itself a mistake. On a flight to Paris on June 1st that year to settle some contracts about 'Goal!' I had met Dany Robin, the French film star, and fallen in love with her. Somehow Lily suspected that there was another woman and that our time together was coming to an end.

Before I went to Greece I had tried to sell the film to the American company Columbia. Its head in Britain, Mo Rothman, had turned it down, but while Lily and I were in Athens I had a call from a Pat Williamson who had just been appointed managing director of Columbia in Mo's place. Pat is English and a football fan.

'I might make a deal over "Goal!" with you,' he told me. 'But first I want to see the footage.'

I arranged to fly back to London on the next plane and Lily drove me to the airport. We both knew it was over between us with having discussed it. As she left me at the airport she said nothing more than: 'Goodbye Michael.'

'Yes, goodbye Lily.'

We did not see each other again until years later when we both were married to other people.

Pat Williamson decided to take 'Goal!'. The picture opened at the Columbia Cinema in London and ran there for ten weeks. Since then Octavio Senoret, Michael Samuelson and I have made a lot of money from it, but I have still never seen a professional football match.

Throughout the entire production of 'Goal!' I never once went to a game and when the film was premiered at the Columbia I went, but was making love to my new girl Dany in the back row. Everyone was too busy watching the movie to take any notice of us, although when they applauded at the end I wondered whose performance they were acknowledging!

Dick Haymes was the possessor of one of the most impressive singing styles in the history of popular music. His phrasing and a timing of a song have been object lessons to thousands of singers, including 'The Guv'nor' himself – Frank Sinatra.

With that talent Dick should have been wealthy and without a worry in the world. But an insatiable thirst for women and booze coupled with an almost dedicated urge for self-destruction were his ruination.

I had not seen him for some years when I took a telephone call in my office from a small-time agent in the East End of London asking if I would be interested in booking Dick Haymes.

'Do you mean Dick Haymes, the American singer, the one who was married to Rita Hayworth?'

Yes, said the man.

'He's an old friend. Please get in touch with him and tell him to ring me.'

Within half an hour Haymes was on the telephone to me. He was staying in Maida Vale, in West London, and I told him to take a taxi and meet me on the corner of Piccadilly and Regent Street.

The last time I had seen Dick was aboard Errol Flynn's

yacht *Zaca* in Jamaica. Then he had been fit, sun-tanned ... and drunk.

He stepped out of the cab that day sober and looking terrible. He was unshaven and a mess, and on the way to my office he told me of his troubles. For a start he was broke and owed the American Government one hundred and thirty five thousand dollars in taxes. He was finding it next to impossible to get work and was living in London.

Haymes needed straightening out and I told him: 'The first thing you do is leave London. Quietly. Go to Paris and I'll let you know when to return. I'll arrange some publicity for your arrival and start getting you some work.'

I provided the air tickets and enough money for him to live on and buy some decent clothes. His 'arrival' in London a few days later wasn't exactly the second coming but it merited enough Press coverage to let people know he was around.

I was still managing Dick Emery and it was easy for me to use Haymes as a special guest star on Dick's TV show.

In rehearsal my old friend was magnificent, singing as well as he had ever done. But the live transmission itself was a disaster. Haymes was as drunk as a fiddler's bitch and an embarrassment to see and hear.

He sang two songs and one of them was 'It Might As Well Be Spring' as far as he was concerned it might have well been 'A Foggy Day In London Town'. He was that smashed.

I dragged him away from the studio muttering all those old cliches like 'pull yourself together' and 'you're letting yourself down' but he was sound asleep next to me in the car.

The rehabilitation of Dick Haymes took many weeks. He was going through a bad patch in his life and the boozing had not helped. The other thing was that he had never really recovered from the collapse of his marriage to Rita Hayworth. He was on top of the world while they were together and after hardly a day passed when he wouldn't talk about her.

His total disregard for his health caught up with him when he contracted tuberculosis and spent more than two months in a hospital in Surrey. During that time I was the only person who visited him – a sad, sorry man with only one friend he could turn to.

Dick came out of hospital, met a model girl called Wendy Smith whom he later married and put his life together again. He still drank but his real boozing sessions were far less frequent than they had been and he started working again.

He was on top form when I had a call from Chequers, the top night club in Sydney, Australia, where they needed someone to head-line their cabaret for the Christmas period.

I sold them Haymes for twelve thousand dollars a week plus two return tickets – one for him, one for me.

My business meant that I couldn't travel on the same flight as Dick and I had arranged to stop over in Perth on the way to Sydney. I arrived there on Christmas Eve and started the trip in style with a crash in my hired car.

Perth is a City where I knew nobody and I couldn't travel to Sydney until Boxing Day. I resigned myself to a lonely Christmas in a hotel room and on Christmas Day I put in calls to Sydney to try to trace Haymes.

When I did contact him he was as lonely as I. 'Rich' I said, 'this is awful. You're there and I'm here and...'

'And we can't even get drunk together,' he cut in.

'That we can. I'll tell you what to do. Put the telephone down and order a load of vodka and a case of tonic water. At this end I'll order scotch and coca-cola then I'll call you back. We'll sit and talk and drink.'

The phone call that followed must have been one of the longest and certainly the drunkest since Edison Bell invented the instrument. Haymes and I talked and drank, drank and talked, all day until we were too drunk to talk any more. There were occasional breaks in our marathon session when we would ring each other back.

At my end the cost of it all came to one hundred and seventy eight pounds and Rich's bill was even higher. All that proves is that he couldn't hold his booze as well as I could and had rung off more frequently!

His opening in Sydney was a huge success and after three weeks I felt that he was doing well enough to be left alone so I caught a flight back to England via Honolulu where I had planned a short holiday.

I had been there for less than a day when I had a call from Sydney. Haymes had been fired the night I left for being drunk on stage so drunk that he had sung (or tried to sing) 'What Kind Of Fool Am I?' thirty six times. The club was threatening to sue him and me and right then I could have told him just what kind of fool he was, in plain old Anglo Saxon.

I had tried and failed to sort him out and I had no intention of going back to Australia, but I felt I could not leave him stranded.

I contacted a solicitor in Sydney and – through him – I managed to settle the matter, but the club flatly refused to have Dick back to complete his engagement. There was no work lined up for him in Britain, so through the same lawyer I managed to keep him busy with some small dates.

When Dick returned to London I had decided that I could not devote half of my life to looking after him. For a while he would behave and then that self-destructive urge would take over.

I knew that Frank Sinatra admired him and had said that he influenced his singing style and career. Dick had also told me that they had always been friendly.

'The man has a reputation for kindness to his friends. Why don't you write to him and see if he can help you get back to the States and sort out your tax problems?' I told Haymes.

He did that and by return he received a cable which told him to collect a pre-paid ticket at Heathrow Airport and fly to Madrid. A hotel reservation had been made for him and he was to stay there and wait for further instructions.

The cabled was signed: 'The King'.

Dick picked up the ticket, flew to Madrid and checked into the hotel where there was an envelope containing two hundred thousand pesetas spending money waiting for him.

He waited a week before the second cable arrived. This one said: 'You are clear with immigration and the tax people. Go to TWA for tickets for you and your family to the U.S. – The King'.

Dick who was by now married to his English girl friend Wendy and had a small child returned to America. He restricted his boozing to white wine and with the help of Sinatra who fixed dates for him at the Ambassador Room in Hollywood, he retrieved his shattered career.

The kindness shown by the often maligned Frank Sinatra had certainly saved a fine talent and a marriage which I am sure would have broken up if Dick had continued to destroy himself.

I never saw Dick Haymes again, although we kept in touch by telephone and the occasional letter and he told me how much he owed to Sinatra.

He died, of cancer, in 1980.

For more than twenty years I have kept quiet about the true facts behind an incident that made a heroine (for a while at least) out of a young film star and almost landed me in jail.

Now I am owning up! The dramatic sea rescue of a young man by Shani Wallis, star of the Oscar-winning film 'Oliver!', was all a great big publicity stunt – and I am the man who engineered it!

In September 1959 headlines around the world told of how Shani had saved the life of a young farm worker Brian Knight when he was drowning off the beach at Brighton, Sussex.

The story went that Shani, then 25, was spending a weekend with friends at Brighton. She went to the beach alone to study the script for her cabaret act. Then, according to Shani at the time:

'I noticed a youth swimming out to sea. I saw him hold one arm up and then disappear. He came up again and I heard him shouting something. The next thing I knew I was in the water, swimming towards him.

'I managed to keep his head above water for a while but my dress of blue knitted wool soaked up the water and weighed like a ton.

'Just as I couldn't hold him up any longer another man reached us. I let go and then I went under myself. The other man was marvellous. Somehow he kept me and the youth afloat and towed us towards the shore.'

The rescued man, 20 year old cowman Brian Knight told

reporters: 'I am certain that but for her I would not be here. She has won herself a fan for life.'

They were both lying in their teeth.

When the fuss had died down Shani received a congratulatory letter from the Mayor of Brighton and there was talk of giving her an award. Modestly the girl said: 'I just wouldn't know where to put it.'

What really happened was that the rescue was a put up job designed to get maximum publicity for Shani, who was starting a month's cabaret engagement at a swanky London Restaurant, the Society, the following day.

For the length of Shani's stay at the Society I thought I had got away with it, but two reporters who were then – and still are – close friends of mine decided that Sullivan had pulled one stroke too many. It took them over a month to nail me and they did it by getting confessions from Brian Knight and the 'amateur photographer' who was supposed to have taken pictures of the rescue.

Even then Shani denied that the rescue was a stunt and I dismissed the confessions as 'fabrication'.

But the police stepped in, statements were taken and a report sent to the Director of Public Prosecutions. Three months after the incident I was called by police officers at Brighton and told they wanted to see me. When I got to Brighton I was told: 'We are going to charge you on a number of counts including misuse of the police, the ambulance service and a few more.

'You'll probably get a five hundred pounds fine and a prison sentence.'

'Do just that,' I told them. 'I'll be pleased if you do charge me. It means that Shani and I will get more publicity... and that is what my business is all about.'

Some time later the Chief Constable of Brighton issued a statement that no action was being taken because 'the evidence does not justify proceedings.'

I dreamed up the rescue stunt because I needed to pull an audience into the Society and to get people talking about Shani. I made the suggestion to Brian O'Hanlon, a young

Irishman who handled publicity for the Society. At first he did not want to know about it, but he did agree to help a little.

Shani used to spend her spare week-ends at the home of music publisher Peter Maurice in Brighton and Brian O'Hanlon's parents also lived in the town.

It was near enough to London to get pictures back quickly and near enough for Shani to return home and wait for the reporters to call.

Brian found, through a publican friend, Brian Knight and on that Sunday morning in Brighton I met Knight and paid him £5 to fake drowning.

I hired a professional photographer to take the pictures to make sure nothing went wrong at that end and then hand the film over to the amateur, Joseph Menozzi, the husband of my former secretary, who would innocently take them to a London news agency.

Once I had paid Knight and settled Shani on the beach with her script I returned to London to wait for Shani.

She opened to a packed house the next night and although it was only natural that some people would suspect that the drowning was a publicity stunt I was convinced I had got away with it.

I reckoned without those two reporters. They were not only friends of mine, they were drinking mates of the weak link in the chain, Brian O'Hanlon. For a month they questioned him, threatened him, persauded him. Brian held firm.

Then they offered money.

In O'Hanlon's case that was the only eventuality I hadn't considered. Maybe I should have paid him.

As it seems to be confession time, here's another: Shani and I were lovers.

I became her manager after I had seen her in a show with comedian Benny Hill at Manchester. We knew each other slightly and she told me: 'I have been wanting you to manage me for years. Can't we talk about it?'

Legally at the time I couldn't act as anybody's manager

because I was bound to an exclusive contract with Shirley Bassey but Shirley and I had parted company while our lawyers fought our battles for us. I was almost broke and needed to do something.

I got around the problem by becoming Shani's 'producer', doing the management job under a different title. I needed to get back in to show business for since parting from Shirley I had been running a strip club called the Keyhole in St James', London, an area renowned for clubs of a vastly different type.

I had owned twenty five per cent of the club for a long time, but when Shirley left I bought out my partners and became the sole owner. I was also flat broke.

My affair with Shani started when I was rehearsing her for her opening at the Society. We worked in her apartment in Irving Street, Leicester Square. I was unhappy because of the break with Shirley and all it was costing me and Shani, a very cute blonde Cockney girl, is one of the world's most warm-hearted people.

She comforted me and that comfort grew into a very emotional affair.

I was still with Lily, my fourth wife at the time and for months Shani and I kept our love secret from her. It was a romance that could have developed into something more, but that old devil of mine – opportunity – stepped in.

Shirley Bassey decided to end our fighting and asked me to start again with her. The night we made up I took Shirley to a restaurant in Chelsea where Shani was dining with record producer Johnny Franz. I broke the news and my Cockney thoroughbred just glared at me and said: 'How can you go back with that *****!

It was all over between us, but Shani went on to much bigger things without me, including the star role as Nancy in 'Oliver!' the British musical which won three Oscars and was nominated for four more.

A few years later Shirley and I parted again. This time for good.

Shani is now very happily married with a family and living in California.

But for Miss Bassey it could have been very different for both of us.

The greatest humiliation to any entertainer is to be paid off... given his money and told he won't be needed any more.

In the days before television killed the variety theatre a bad reception for an act on the opening night often meant that it was paid off on a Tuesday. Apart from the shame for the act it never reflected too well on the booker who had arranged the date. Too many paid off artists meant that he, too, would soon be out of work.

As a booker I had only three acts paid off. At the time it hurt, but when I look back on those incidents I console myself with the thought that my three 'failures' were... Norman Wisdom, Harry Secombe and Peter Sellers!

Norman 'died' at The Grand Theatre, Blackburn; Harry met his Waterloo at another Grand – in Bolton – and Peter's came much nearer home in London at the Palace, East Ham.

They were all acts earning around twenty five or thirty pounds a week. It was my luck to be handling them then – not when their earnings had soared into the thousands!

After that magnificent foursome The Goons had split I became Michael Bentine's agent, but my acquaintance with them all goes back to the days before they completely rewrote the book of British humour with their oustandingly successful radio shows.

At the time I was living in the Mapleton Hotel in London, which was nothing like as grand as it might sound. I was a struggling agent, trying to build a business in the immediate post-war days, and the Goons were no better off.

There have been times when we all sat around in my small room in the Mapleton, clubbed together to have two orders of spaghetti sent up and split it five ways.

Apart from Michael Bentine, one of the easiest clients I ever handled, I saw little of the other Goons after they had become star names, but Peter Sellers and I both fell for the same woman... and I married her.

In 1969 I was married for the fifth (and definitely the last) time to a beautiful French film actress Dany Robin. Seven years earlier Peter tried to woo her when they worked together in Britain on the film 'The Waltz Of The Toreadors'.

One evening Dany accepted an invitation to his flat in Hampstead. She had no idea what to expect, but convinced that she could handle Peter, went along.

Once he had got her inside the flat Peter got to work with his seduction technique... by showing her FOUR of his own films, one after the other!

The lady did not succumb.

ACT TWO
Scene One: Dick Emery

As I walked out of a London bank my path crossed with that of the owner of a dozen of the best-known faces in Britain. I smiled and took a step forward. He stopped and stiffened.

'Dick! It's been a long time. How are you?'

'Hello, Michael.' The voice matched the expression, flat and cold.

'Got time for a drink? Let's have a talk.'

'No thank you Michael. I don't think we have anything to talk about.'

The late Dick Emery, comic genius and one of the most perplexing human beings I have ever known, walked on.

There was a time when that meeting would not have been by chance and would have been full of affection, but in a business where it is easy to bear grudges Dick Emery had chosen to cut me out of his life, prepared not to forget what caused us to part but to forget the closeness that had existed between us.

Dick once wrote me a beautiful letter which read: 'I will never leave you. You made me a star...' I will risk being labelled as immodest by saying that the second statement is absolutely correct.

For ten years I worked on and with Dick to cultivate the enormous talent he had. From it we both earned a lot of money, but for my share of it I often had to live two lives simultaneously – mine and his.

I first realised Dick's talent when I watched him rehearsing at the BBC-TV Centre in West London in 1962. He was appearing regularly in the Michael Bentine series 'It's a

Square World' and I was staggered by his amazing changes of character.

Convinced that he could be a major star, I walked over to him, using the name of the powerful Delfont agency of which I was a director, and introduced myself. I also reminded him that in the nineteen thirties I had booked him for one pound ten shillings a time on Friday night cine-variety bills and invited him to lunch the next day.

We met at Tolaini's Restaurant in Wardour Street, Soho, and there I offered him a five-year agency and management contract and promised him his own BBC-TV series. The deal, which meant he would part with twenty per cent of his earnings, would not be signed until the series was confirmed.

Dick had nothing to lose and agreed to the deal, providing he got that series. I went back to my office and telephoned Tom Sloan, the BBC's head of TV light entertainment and told him I would like to see him.

Tom and I made a date for the following Monday and I told Dick to meet me at the TV Centre then.

When I walked into Tom's office Dick was at my side. The BBC man had not expected this nor did he expect my opening line:

'Tom, would you agree that this man here is almost the foundation stone of "It's A Square World"?'

'Yes. I suppose so.'

'Then why doesn't he have his own series. The BBC is a public corporation using public money. Here is a very original talent and you are taking that public money under false pretences if you allow him to go to commercial television.' I went on in the same vein for some time.

When Dick and I left that office we had a thirteen part TV series for him. When that contract was signed Dick signed himself to me and our association began.

He brought me more problems than any male entertainer I have ever handled. Every agent has to put up with some of the anguish of his clients' private lives, but with Dick his private existence and his professional one were inextricably mixed. The first was, on a daily basis, a total shambles and it consistently interfered with his work.

Dick's fifth wife, actress and dancer Josephine Blake, once told me: 'If you live with Dick Emery you live with half a dozen characters and you have to find out who's who'.

That isn't a problem only his wives and friends have. I am convinced that a lot of the time Dick wasn't quite sure just who he was.

He was an extraordinarily complex man, a mixture of paradoxes that hide the real human being. He was both generous and at the same time incredibly mean; he was a supreme egotist, yet feared rejection; he believed himself to be a sincere person but his sincerity was just a veneer (although he was not aware of this); he was a dedicated womaniser who had an unfounded terror of homosexuality; he had an enormous sense of humour and was hopelessly insecure and unhappy at times.

The great problem in Dick's life was always women. He was a man who didn't like the company of other men and had little rapport with them. In spite of his womanising he would never talk of his conquests. He was not the sort of man to go into a pub for a pint – he preferred a much more sophisticated life in the company of women.

When we met and agreed to work together he was engaged to a pretty red-haired girl called Vicki. Two years later they married and he bought her a boutique at Cobham in Surrey, but even while they were planning their wedding Dick was chasing other girls.

After getting him his own TV series I fixed him to play the part of the cat in the pantomime 'Dick Whittington' at the London Palladium. Also in the cast was a lovely comedienne called Audrey Jeans. Dick was immediately attracted to her (in fact, he was immediately attracted to all women) and before long they were lovers.

Unfortunately for Dick, Audrey was the girl friend of a very important and kindly man in the entertainment business. He had suspected their affair and one evening he sent his assistant to the Palladium to find out what was going on.

This bright young man did not take long to confirm all of his boss's suspicions and went back to him with the news.

In other circumstances it would have been one of those everyday romantic triangles, but this time, because of the people involved, it became a serious threat to a lot of business relationships... most of them mine.

Powerful colleagues suggested that the best move I could make was to cancel my contract with Dick. Either that or move into another area of show business.

I agreed to neither and explained that we were all in the business of entertainment and the object was to be successful. Personal relationships between two acts should not affect us and I could hardly be expected to be responsible for Dick's love affairs.

On the side I got hold of Dick and told him: 'You have just got your own TV series. You are on your way and you're ruining everything over a bird. Just find somebody else. I don't care who, but not her.'

He saw sense, stopped the affair and started chasing another girl.

Dick married Vicki in 1964 and some time later he was repaid for his philandering in a way that hurt him more than anything else I knew.

He was appearing in a summer show in Blackpool and after the curtain came down one evening he decided – guided by some suspicious sixth sense – to check up on Vicki. He drove at terrific speed in his Bentley to Cobham, rushed into the house and found her with a boy friend.

To somebody with Dick's ego the scene was shattering. He left the house and telephoned me at my home in Denham, Bucks.

'Mike, I know the time, but I have got to see you. Right away.'

He sounded in a very bad way and I asked him to come to the house. He refused and said he wanted to meet me in the middle of Denham village because what he wanted to discuss he didn't want Lily, my wife, to hear.

When we met about three thirty in the morning he was in

tears. 'How could she do this to me? I am mad about her', he sobbed as he told me of the scene at Cobham.

I persuaded him to come home with me and spent the rest of the night talking to him. I took the middle path and pointed out that Vicki's fling was only to be expected after the way he had behaved with other women.

'She hasn't been blind, Dick. How do you expect a girl to put up with what you have been doing?' I said. 'Go home, forgive her and make it up.'

Dick and Vicki patched up their marriage, with Dick (I am sure) swearing eternal fidelity. At the time he was really sincere about it – but within three days he was having an affair with a chorus girl from the Blackpool show.

Dick's obsession with women was endless. He was completely indiscriminate in choice – type, shape, colour or looks made no difference to him – and he would pursue a girl of his fancy with an embarrassing fervour.

He loved working with pretty girls and spent a lot of his time during breaks in rehearsals chatting to them, trying to date them, squeezing and patting them. It was as if touching them was some sort of hourly test he put himself to, a test to make sure he would not be rejected.

Maybe much of what troubled him can be traced to his young days. Dick was, to use an old show business phrase, 'born in a basket', the child of a theatrical couple and has known nothing but the business from infancy.

He had a very unhappy childhood and told me how he grew up detesting his father for the way in which he treated his mother. As a result he was always very good to his mother and would never fail to visit her in her flat near Marble Arch, London, two or three times a week.

It is perhaps this affection for his mother that always made him want to be with women rather than men. His romances and affairs caused me many headaches and the worst was when he was threatened by a blackmailing pimp.

Dick came into my office shaken and worried stiff one day. 'Mike, I have got into trouble. Just do something – anything – to get me out of it.'

He explained that on his way home at night to Surrey he would drive through the Shepherds Bush area of West London. Late one night he had stopped there and picked up a black girl – a whore.

'I paid her, and she knew who I was,' he said. 'Now I have had a man on to me. He says he's her husband and that she's pregnant. He wants three thousand pounds. What are we going to do?'

We? It was his pleasure, now when the going gets rough it's 'We'!

'Dick, WE are going to do nothing. I am going to get in touch with David and see what he says.'

I telephoned my lawyer David Jacobs, a shrewd, flamboyant homosexual who later committed suicide, and discussed the matter with him.

On David's advice I agreed to meet the 'husband' of the girl and took with me a cheque signed 'Michael Sullivan'.

I met the man in a cafe near Shepherd's Bush and we talked about the pay off. Talking deals has been my life. Pimping on cheap hookers was his. He didn't stand a chance.

Before I handed over the cheque which I had talked him into accepting rather than money I had discovered his name and address and had called there to make sure he was telling the truth.

Then I left him clutching the cheque and went to the local police station. I gave a C.I.D. officer David Jacob's telephone number and after explaining what had happened, left.

The following morning I cancelled the cheque and left everything to David. Apart from the bill for his services neither Dick nor I heard another word on the subject.

That experience should have quietened Dick down, or at the very least put a brake on his lust, but it did not.

He had met Josephine Blake, a superb dancer and very good comedy 'feed', while in a show at the Prince of Wales Theatre in London. Jo – a leggy blonde, much taller than Dick – also worked in a couple of sketches on his TV series and appeared in a summer show with him.

The inevitable happened and once again it was tear-time

for Vicki, who by now had two young children.

At all times of the night I was called in by one or other of them, Dick and Vicki, to mediate in the bitter rows they were having over Jo.

Dick's problem was that he just did not know when to cut loose. He wanted Jo, but he also wanted Vicki – and he couldn't have both.

A typical example of his insecurity showed itself during this period. He was due to work in Australia and *had* to take a woman with him. He could not make up his mind whether it should be Vicki or Jo and booked tickets on the flight in both of their names. Up until the very last moment he was still deciding... but Jo won and went with him.

The marriage to Vicki ended in divorce in 1968 and for a man with his money Dick got off very lightly. Under the terms of the divorce settlement Vicki got the house and the shop in Cobham and a few thousand pounds with no regular alimony. In addition Dick paid for the education of their two children.

The next year he married Jo. Their wedding was a very small and – for me – sad affair.

They married on a Saturday morning at a register office and celebrated it with lunch at the Fairmile Hotel near Esher. Only six other people attended that lunch: Jo's mother and brother, comedian Jack Douglas and his wife Sue and my wife Dany and I. Dick had not even asked Dany and I to go to the register office. I have always felt that Dick's lack of friends was poignantly illustrated on that day.

Soon after the wedding the rows with Jo started and once again I was called in as the peacemaker.

At first I didn't like Jo very much. I thought she pushed herself forward too hard and would give me problems. But the more I was dragged into their disputes the more I sympathised with her and grew fond of her.

The trouble between them started because Dick wanted Jo to give up work and in this I think he was following my lead. He had always seemed to do what I did. If I bought something he would do the same – like the time I bought a

Rolls Royce and he sold his Bentley to buy one.

I had never wanted Dany to work and Dick took the same line with Jo. Unlike Dany, Jo objected, but he wore her down and managed, most of the time, to keep her as a housewife at their home on St George's Hill, Weybridge, in Surrey.

I found it hard not to side with Jo in their battles, but my first loyalty was to Dick. I told him: 'My position as your friend and your manager is simple – if you are happy I am happy. But just make up your mind.'

I learned just how inflated that ego was the night that Dick tried to make love... to my daughter!

From my first marriage I have two children, Michelle and Nicolette, now both in their thirties. I had not seen them since they were babies aged three and one when I received a call from Michelle, the eldest. She was at her mother's home in Great Yarmouth, and the girls were then in their twenties.

She and her sister were going to live in Australia and decided that they ought to see their father just once before they left Britain for good.

I needed help with this situation and I called on Dick. When the two girls, both complete strangers to me, stepped off the train at Liverpool Street station, London, he was there with me to greet them.

Together we took them shopping, then for lunch in the West End. We all went to a matinee of a London Palladium pantomime and then for drinks at my house in Esher, Surrey.

I had booked a table at the Fairmile Hotel for us and Dick drove the party there. After dinner he drove us back to the house and Nicolette and I, who had shared the back seat of his car got out and went in. We waited for Dick and Michelle but after about ten minutes I went to the door to find out if there was trouble with car.

Michelle walked in followed by Dick, smiling and cracking jokes. My daughter drew me to one side and as Dick went into the sitting room she told me:

'That Mr Emery is a terrible man. He kept grabbing me and putting his hand up my leg. He wanted to drive off up the road with me, but I wouldn't have it.'

Later when the girls had gone to bed (they were staying for two nights before flying out) I tackled Dick about his behaviour.

'Did you mean it Dick, or were you just joking? Tell me you were just horsing around.'

'I wasn't joking. I meant it Michael. I really fancy her.'

'But Dick, that girl is my daughter. How could you?'

He was completely unruffled.

'She may be your daughter Michael, but she's very attractive.'

The man was impossible!

One of things about his public image that worried Dick most was the effect his female characters and those 'camp' expressions like 'hello sailor' might have on it.

It is a fact that a lot of the people who saw him on TV wondered about his sexuality. And Dick knew it.

Because of this he had a pathological fear of any taint of homosexuality. He knew that some people thought he was gay, but the awful vision that he might actually have any tendencies in that direction haunted him.

I tried often to reassure him that he was not going to wake up one morning and find that he had changed. He had nothing to worry about, but worry he did and this may account for his relentless pursuit of women . . . a man trying to show the world and, more importantly, himself that he is totally heterosexual.

When I first signed a contract with Dick Emery he was earning one hundred and twenty pounds a week. Six months later this had risen to five hundred and at his peak he could count his weekly earnings in thousands.

We had earned so much money together that I suppose it was inevitable that it should be the cause of our parting.

While I was away from the office a young man who was working there and learning the agency business took a call from a company who wanted Dick to appear at a private dinner. They had one thousand pounds to spend and were told that for that money Dick would entertain them for the evening.

It is fairly common practice when an agent books a complete cabaret for him to charge a fee for the 'package' and then try to cream off an extra profit by keeping the total sum paid to the various artists below the figure he is getting.

But when you are dealing with just one artist that practice is not only unethical... it is bordering on the criminal and for doing it an agent could lose his licence.

The man in my office told Dick that he would be getting seven hundred and fifty pounds for the date, but when he had performed at the dinner the organiser approached him with his fee – one thousand pounds!

Dick was furious. He issued writs on London Management, the agency of which I was a director, and his solicitor threatened to report the agency to the Great London Council.

Our licence was in jeopardy and although I had already received a letter from Dick telling me that our association was over I went from London to Southampton, where he was appearing on an old contract, to see him.

I begged him to drop the writs and the complaint for the sake of people at the agency who had nothing to do with the incident. 'It is my responsibility and mine alone – even though I wasn't there,' I said.

Dick graciously agreed to end the matter, but in the circumstances there was nothing I could do except resign from the board of London Management. I was unhappy and disillusioned and moved to Spain.

Later I was back in London on a visit when I heard that Dick was in hospital with a heart tremor. I rang Josephine at their home and was told: 'He doesn't want to see you or speak to you and as far as I am concerned he is in hospital because of you.'

I hung up, but in 1980 when Dick had left Jo for his latest chorus girl I called her and offered any help I could give.

During our conversation she broke down and said: 'I wish you were still his manager Mike, but it's too late now. It has gone beyond even your help.'

Until that meeting in a London street with Dick I had hoped that it wasn't the case...

Scene Two: 'Carry On Trying'

The golden rule in show business is: 'If it succeeds... flog it to death', and nowhere is this better demonstrated than in the film business, James Bond, Tarzan, Sherlock Holmes, Charlie Chan – these characters have been bled dry once it has been established that people will pay money to see them.

But no cinema concept has ever become an institution of the same dimensions as the 'Carry On' films. Their banal, suggestive plots and scripts have established them as a cult form.

Made on shoe-string budgets and tailored so that they would recoup their total production costs in Britain, the films are one of the cinemas most extraordinary success stories.

Since producer Peter Rogers and director Gerald Thomas made 'Carry On Sergeant' in 1958 they churned them out at the rate of about two a year.

And I almost brought their gravy train to a halt!

After I had become manager to Sidney James I also signed agency contracts with actors Charles Hawtrey and Kenneth Connor. All three were 'Carry On' stalwarts and their representation gave me quite a lot of unseen power in the making of the films.

I tried time and again to woo Joan Sims and Kenneth Williams to let me act as their agent but I could never persuade them to join me. Had that been possible I would have had a virtual stranglehold on the productions – a situation that could have earned me a fortune – but it was not to be and I remained satisfied with my lot...

Until Leslie Grade who was the chairman of the agency of

which I was a director, started to make a film deal with the American distributors United-Artists.

Here I saw all the makings of a method to bring the 'Carry Ons' into our fold and I succeeded in talking Peter and Gerald into leaving the Anglo-Amalgamated company run by Nat Cohen and coming to us.

At a meeting between the two film makers, Leslie and myself one Friday the deal was confirmed. I had broken new ground and was already thinking of the profits.

But because show business, more than any other is a world of personalities it was not to be. On the Saturday Leslie Grade had a heart attack and without him United Artists would not go ahead with their side of the deal with the agency. Maybe they had wanted a way out, maybe they held Leslie in such high regard that they were being honest about having no deal without his personal participation. I will never know.

What I do know is that the situation left the 'Carry On' films hanging in the balance. Peter and Gerald could not go back to Nat Cohen for a distribution deal and all I could do was apologise.

It took Peter Rogers some months before he did manage to sign a contract with the Rank Organisation to handle his films and by then I had lost a lot of face, a lot of faith and a lot of the clout I once had in the productions.

Scene Three: The Funny Men

Funny men (funny on stage, that is, because privately so many comedians are anything but amusing and lovable) have been as much a part of my life as my many wives.

They have brought me money, heartache and some wonderful triumphs and the deaths in the past couple of years of Dick Emery, Tommy Cooper and Eric Morecambe have been tragic losses to our business of keeping the paying public happy and entertained.

They ALL brought sunshine into our hearts and have provided me with a hatful of irreplacable memories.

When Dick Emery died I had just left a Spanish hospital after a serious operation and had been ordered not to travel. I could not go to Dick's funeral and the card on the wreath I sent, for me at any rate, said it all:

'At last you can rest in peace.'

True emotional serenity was something that Dick never knew in his life and the arguments between his wife and his last girl friend that followed his death were horrendous.

I was told that they even fought over who should have his ashes... let alone his money and this black comedy appealed so much to my sense of humour that I told a friend:

'They ought to form cricket teams and play for them each year'.

If that sounds crude, I can tell you that – in the days when we were friends – Dick would have appreciated it as the sort of remark he had come to expect from me.

Tommy Cooper was a totally different man from Dick and I don't believe that there was any such thing as a 'dark' side to his nature. He worked for me often, but aside from business our relationship extended only as far as being occasional drinking buddies... especially in the days when I ran a club in the St James's area of London.

Tommy loved a drink and even back in the Sixties would spend as much as seventy five and eighty pounds a night at my bar. In fact, I got so concerned at his bills that I ordered the barman never to give him a bill of more than fifty pounds.

His comedy magic routines brought Tommy the public recognition he deserved, but aside from the hilarious fumbled tricks he was one of the funniest men in the business. I have seen audiences almost paralysed with laughter without him saying a single word or doing a thing.

He had that wonderful art of just looking as though he didn't know where he was or what he was doing – and it was more than enough to get laughs. He was a clown with an unmistakable magic of his own.

Eric Morecambe and Ernie Wise were turned down by me when I was mounting the pantomime 'Babes In The Wood' and their agent, Frank Pope, suggested them for the two robbers in the production, but when, in 1950, I was involved in another panto at the Empire Theatre in Dewsbury I promised Frank I would take the producer, Reg Bolton, along to see them where they were working in Chester.

Reg was undoubtedly one of the best authorities on pantomime comedy in Britain and after seeing Eric and Ernie he said he could provide them with all the 'bits' that would make them worth booking.

Frank Pope, whose main function in life was booking a small circuit of theatres and representing just one act, Morecambe and Wise, fought with me about money and their billing and after the end of the show's sixteen week run at Dewsbury, and with all of Reg Bolton's expert advice behind them, they were on their way.

Frank Pope was a man of some vision. He could see that the advance of television would mean the end of live variety and he fought long and hard to break down barriers and get his act their own TV series.

He finally managed it with the BBC, but once the pair were truly established they decided that their new and bigger career demanded a new and bigger agent.

As soon as their contract with Frank ran out, they left him and he – broken-hearted – left the business.

This wasn't the only time that the pair didn't spread any sunshine. When Bill Cotton Jnr was appointed head of light entertainment for BBC television there were just two shows a week with a variety content. Within two years Bill had changed this and there were sixteen.

One of them was the Morecambe and Wise show and after a disappointing start new writers, directors and producers came up with a format that made Eric and Ernie the biggest comedy property in the country.

They repaid Bill by switching to ITV at the very height of their popularity.

But that is the way of show business and in spite of it I have one wonderful memory of Eric and Ernie in the days when the giant Grade Organisation, which represented so many stars, became a public company.

The pair were under contract to the organisation and were agented by one of its directors, Billy Marsh.

Leslie Grade was presenting a summer show at the ABC Theatre in Blackpool and wanted Eric and Ernie to appear in it. But he would not pay them more than two thousand pounds a week and Billy could not get them to accept.

Finally a meeting was arranged with Leslie and the outcome was that they signed a contract for two thousand five hundred.

As they left the office Eric looked at Leslie and told him: 'I want you to know that Ernie and I are shareholders in the Grade Organisation and you pay your stars too much money for summer shows!'

Jimmy Wheeler was, right up until his death in 1973, one of the best-loved comedians in the variety world, and one of his greatest performances should never have taken place!

At the time he was working for me at the Empire Theatre, Nottingham. There was also in the same town a Theatre

Royal and the two places were connected by an underground tunnel.

Now Jimmy was a lush, but he never let the booze interfere with his performance... even if he was in the wrong place.

One night, before he was due to do his second show, he left his dressing room and turned left instead of right down that tunnel.

He finished up in the wings of the Theatre Royal, heard applause, saw the stage was empty and presumed that the previous act had taken their curtain call. Jimmy stepped on that stage and went straight into his routine.

Later he told me that it had never gone better – even though he was in the wrong theatre and appearing at the end of the second half of the ballet 'Sleeping Beauty'!

One comedian for whom I hold an extra special affection and respect is Jimmy Tarbuck, both as a performer and a person.

I have known Tarby for many years and for three of them he worked exclusively for me in summer shows. Now after a career that has had its ups and downs he's right on top of the game... thanks to the astute Michael Parkinson putting him on his TV chat show.

The rapport between the two of them was a sheer joy to watch and from then on he has gone from strength to strength.

But the private side of Tarbuck is one worthy of tribute, too.

I have lived in Marbella in Southern Spain for 12 years now and some time ago I felt I should do something for the local community and started to run golf competitions to raise money for handicapped children.

The man who helped me more than anyone else was Jimmy. He sold raffle tickets in any restaurant he walked into on his frequent trips to Marbella and he helped me muster some great fields of competitors.

Once when Jimmy and I were playing a four ball at the El Paraiso course in Marbella with Sean Connery and another friend, we reached the sixteenth tee from where you can see my garden.

Sean looked across and saw my wife Dany's two grandchildren playing there and said: 'You have three children, don't you Mike?'

'Yes. Two married and in Australia and a son who roams the world as an electrician with theatre companies.'

'I thought you didn't like kids,' Sean continued.

'I don't. Not even my own.'

Tarby then butted in with: 'You should have tied your wedding tackle in a knot.'

'I tried – but it was always too stiff!'

They broke up with laughter and hit what must have been the worst drives of their golfing careers.

Tarby's timing of a gag is impeccable and at a London golfing dinner in 1982 he even stole the show from his idol Bob Hope, but if I were guiding his career now I would insist that he moved away from being a 'stand up' comic. And that advice goes for so many of the comedic talents we have in Britain.

If only our agents, writers and producers would take note of the careers of great American funnymen such as Hope, George Burns, Red Skelton and Phil Silvers they would realise that a switch to situation comedy – both in films and TV – is essential.

Performances like that of George Burns in 'The Sunshine Boys'; Bob Hope in the 'Road' series with Crosby; Phil Silvers' marvellous 'Bilko', still being shown on British TV, and Red Skelton's comedy films for M.G.M. have all shown how having the wisdom to turn down immediate big money in their own spheres in order to succeed on the screen has paid enormous dividends.

The same principle applies to singers, as Crosby, Sinatra, Doris Day and Elvis Presley have all shown.

This is the age of screen entertainment. The old style variety techniques may provide the grounding for a great act, but they can never again sustain an entertainer at the very top of his profession.

I would dearly love to see Jimmy Tarbuck and Des O'Connor in a situation comedy and the idea of Tarby and Kenny Lynch in an English version of 'The Odd Couple' would be pure magic.

When I first went to live in Spain I was sad and a little embittered by show business, but if I was really trying to escape from it in Marbella I picked the wrong place.

A few years ago it was like living on California's Malibu Beach. There were so many stars around.

Deborah Kerr, Stewart Granger, Mel Ferrer, Madeleine Carroll, Ray Milland, Sean Connery and a stack of others were all fairly near neighbours and with some I became very friendly.

Mel Ferrer, however, did not fall into that category. He came just once to my house to offer Dany a part in a film he was producing and as he walked arrogantly into the place he stared around at the antiques we have taken so much trouble to collect and sneered:

'It's like a museum.'

As I turned on my heel and walked out I retorted: 'And now we've got another piece to exhibit!'

Ferrer's co-star in the swashbuckling film 'Scaramouche' was Stewart Granger, a totally different and thoroughly lovable and likeable character.

During his time in Marbella 'Jimmy' Granger didn't exactly endear himself to the jet setters there, but, then, he has never suffered fools gladly.

Dany and I became good friends with him and we often visited his magnificent house in the Andalusian mountains.

Jimmy had travelled all over Spain finding old doors, archways, stone and wooden chimneys and other antiquities for the place and I have never seen such good taste in decoration. The man loves cooking and he would come to our villa to watch a film on the video and bring all the ingredients for a steak tartare with him.

But in spite of all the good things he had surrounded himself with he was so often deeply sad and never seemed to stop talking of his Jean (Jean Simmons, the lovely English star to whom he was once married).

One evening he suddenly switched off the video machine and turned to Dany and I and said: 'Imagine, in five minutes I will be celebrating my sixty fifth birthday and my son Jamie is in London.' As he switched the film on again I winked to Dany and beckoned her to the kitchen. We found a cake, stuck an enormous candle in the centre of it and parcelled up a picture. Precisely at midnight we threw the main light switch and danced into the room singing 'Happy Birthday'.

Jimmy Granger cried like a baby.

Later when I heard that his autobiography was being published I left a congratulatory note at our local barber shop with another piece of paper which read 'This entitles you to a transplant or four free haircuts... by arrangement with Michael Sullivan.'

He repaid me as I was recovering from a prostate gland operation recently with a cable from California, where he now lives, which read: 'Have this one on me. You've rehearsed the prostrate position often enough.'

In my early days as an agent I worked in partnership with a man called Jack D. Roberton, one of the old breed of show businessmen. Running around our office at the time, giving his father and I a hand by making the tea and carrying messages was Jack's youngest son, Jack Junior.

Over the years the Robertons and I kept in touch and old Jack' elder boy Bill worked with me in the years immediately before I left London for good.

Young Jack, in the meantime, had stayed in the business but had moved on to the performing side and in 1968 he was 'feeding' Des O'Connor on stage and on TV. His television appearances with Des as the twitching loon Jack Ippytittimus had established a trade mark for him, but I never realised how popular he was until – with Bill Roberton – I attended a Royal Variety Performance.

The Barron Knights, a talented group who combined comedian with songs, featured Jack's character in their 'royal' act and as we watched I turned to Bill and said:

'We haven't realised it, but your brother's a star. The fact that the Knights are "doing" him shows that. People recognise him.'

At the time I had started putting Sidney James into touring

plays and thought that the same formula could work with other comics.

I called Jack where he was working in Glasgow and told him I was sending a ticket to Belfast to him as there was something I wanted him to see.

He had no idea what I had planned but turned up in Belfast on schedule.

I took him to see a play called 'Don't Tell The Wife' and after he had sat quietly through it he asked me:

'So?'

'So, would you like to star in it?'

'Do you mean that?'

I meant it and later that year Jack opened in the play at Oxford where it was tried out for a week before it went into a record-breaking summer season at Blackpool.

From then on Jack's money soared to one thousand pounds a week, and he became one of the most popular funny men on British TV.

And it had taken brother Bill and I nearly twenty years to realise that our office boy had talents that extended far, far beyond licking the stamps and making tea.

Jack, for all his humour, can be a very serious man and he has a great sense of formality and occasion. Scots comedian Jimmy Logan played on this for a small practical joke at a dinner party one evening.

I telephoned Jack and invited him and his wife Sue to dinner at my place, explaining that Jimmy would also be there.

'You know I wouldn't do this normally, Jack,' I said, 'but Logan believes in dressing properly for everything. He'll be there in all the Highland gear – kilt, the lot. So make sure Sue and yourself are in the right clothes. We don't want to offend Jimmy.'

When Jack and Sue turned up at my home he was in dinner jacket and bow tie and Sue wore her newest and loveliest long evening dress.

The rest of sat down to dinner, ideally dressed for a very hot summer's evening in casual clothes!

The sweltering Douglasses are – I'm sure – still waiting for a chance to get their own back.

Old girl friends – and wives – have often been remarkably helpful to me in my life, and one of them was responsible for virtually handing me on a plate one of the most successful TV series in Britain.

Duncan Wood, the head of light entertainment for Yorkshire TV is an old friend with whom I have often played golf in Spain. Over one game he asked me:

'Mike, we need a good game show at Yorkshire. Keep your eyes open and try to find one for us. You could be on to a good thing.'

I was involved in a lot of travelling at the time and wherever I went around the world I scouted for a show that might fit his requirements. I came up with nothing. Zero.

Back home on the Costa del Sol I met up with a delightful American lady, Esmeralda, who used to be part of a cycling act, the New Dolly Sisters. She was also an old girl friend of mine.

We talked about old times, old friends and what we were both doing. I explained that I was looking for a show... a game show, but couldn't find one.

'Take a look at "Uno-Dos-Tres",' said Esmeralda. 'It's the biggest thing in Spain.'

Even my knowledge of the language of my adopted country reaches far enough to know that the title means 'One-Two-Three', but with my command of Spanish it is never worthwhile looking at a local programme.

With a Spanish-speaking friend at my side I watched the hour and half long show, had it explained to me and then called Duncan.

He came to Spain and it took four months of negotations before I acquired the British rights to the show and then sold them to Yorkshire TV.

'Three-Two-One' has been in the higher spots of the British TV ratings ever since it started now and it has also made a big star of its compere, comedian Ted Rogers, and enabled me to keep a promise I made to Ted when I first met him on a Bing Crosby show in New York.

I was so impressed with his humour that I told him: 'If I ever get the right sort of vehicle I'll hand it to you.'

What I never realised was that after travelling half way round the world looking for it, I would find it on my own doorstep.

The profit margin in the 'legitimate' theatre has always been too narrow to attract me, but even I could see the possibilities of bringing the Bolshoi Ballet to England and when Dany's sister Collette mentioned the chance of a deal through a choreographer friend I jumped.

The choreographer, a French woman called Verina Boccadoro had been working with the Bolshoi in Moscow and she asked Collette if her brother-in-law would be interested in presenting 'Amour pour Amour', a loose adaptation of Shakespeare's 'Much Ado About Nothing' in England.

At the time the Bolshoi Ballet was on a limited tour of France and in November 1980 Dany and I drove from Paris to Lyon to see the production. Much to my wife's disgust, I have never been a ballet enthusiast. I don't like the way the dancers contort themselves and I've never fancied women who walk with the feet splayed in that 'ten to two' position!

But after the evening in Lyon I turned to Dany and said: 'There must be something wrong. I actually enjoyed it.'

I was so impressed that I was determined to present the Bolshoi and a meeting was arranged for the following day with the director of the company, the choreographer and three men who looked as though they knew more about coal mining than ballet dancing... there, presumably, to make sure no-one defected.

The outcome of that meeting was that I arranged to go to Moscow to discuss the finer details with Gosconcert, the Russian government agency which controls the Bolshoi and the renowned Moscow State Circus.

It took weeks to get visas processed for Dany and myself, but that December we arrived in Russia, and for ten days it looked as though the old show business agent's saying 'Don't call us, we'll call you' had, at last, rebounded upon me.

We just sat and waited and every evening we went to the ballet.

Even the interpreter who had been arranged for us began to look embarrassed, but finally the call came and I settled down to business with the men of Gosconcert.

At the end I knew a lot about the Bolshoi, but still didn't have a deal. It took five more trips to Moscow before I came out with a contract for a six week tour of Britain and a six week season in London. I threatened to present the Bolshoi Defectors!

And then, just as it was all coming together, Russia invaded Afghanistan and screwed up everything.

I've still got the contract, the deal with Bolshoi is still on ice, but I'm terrified that if I ever try to finalise it there's bound to be another international incident.

How can a bastard win on the legitimate side of the fence?

A four-ball golf competition between left to right, Bill Richmond, Sean Connery, Pat Ryan and myself, who was already de-balled and laughing with Eric Sykes before we teed off.

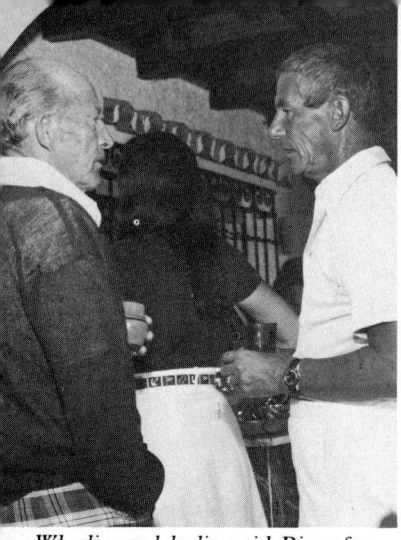

Wheeling and dealing with Bing after I had allowed him to win the round of golf. Dean Martin — I hate him because my wife loves him! A reunion with Kirk and Anne Douglas at their home in Palm Springs.

Marilyn Monroe and I sat in the bedroom just hoping it would work.

Did Bruce really find the ladies "a drag"? Ava Gardner — The Lady Who Came to Dinner.

Kathy Kirby, a great talent pursued by ill fate. Bogart always did as he pleased including blacking my eye — don't do it again Sam!

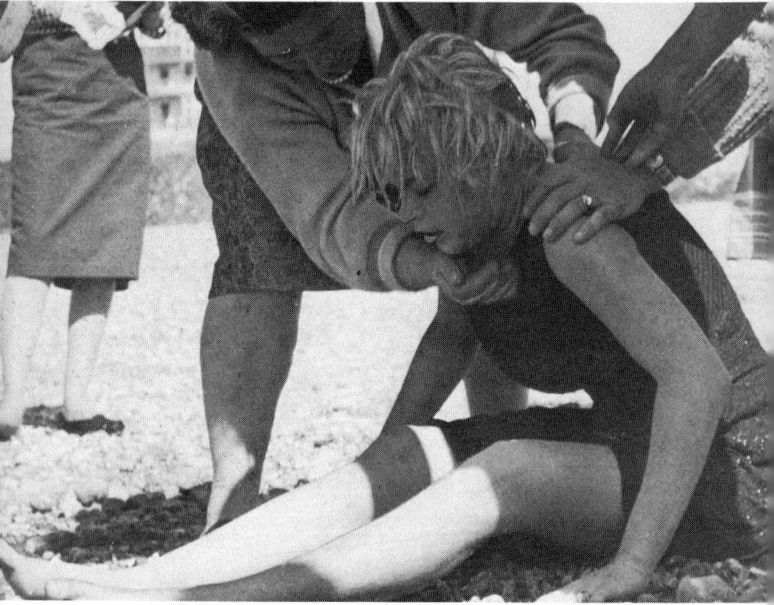

Shani Wallis a rare and exciting talent and a very beautiful woman and the publicity gag that backfired and put Shani's life at stake for the sake of "Cafe Society".

Dany Robin in the company of Claudia Cardinale, Pat Boone and Peter Sellers, being presented to Her Royal Highness Queen Elizabeth II on the occasion of the film, The Waltz of the Toreadors, having been chosen as the Royal Command film.

Laughter is the joy of life but sometimes it was hard with Dick, hence the mask above my head. Tarby — a friend indeed.

Scene Four: The Power Men

If ever a handful of men held the reins and purse strings of British show business from the years just after the Second World War until well into the 'Swinging Sixties' they were Jack Hylton, Val Parnell and those three magnificent brothers – the Grades.

When commercial television arrived in Britain in 1956 their power became almost absolute: Val and Lew Grade were firmly in control of Associated TeleVision, providing week-day programmes for the Midlands and also the contractors for London week-ends; Jack, the tough little ex-bandleader from Lancashire, ruling his own particular roost from the Victoria Palace theatre with the Crazy Gang; Leslie Grade and the third of Mrs Winogradski's boys, Bernard Delfont, controlling the country's biggest agency, the Grade Organisation.

In addition Jack Hylton had a contract to provide a regular variety show and a number of 'specials' each year for the London week-day TV company, Associated-Redifusion.

What place could the trivia of petty feuds have in the lives of such Olympians?

In the case of Val Parnell and Jack Hylton, a huge and bitter one.

There had been a vendetta between the two master showmen for years and at the centre of it were seven of the greatest clowns in history – Bud Flanagan, Chesney Allen, Jimmy Nervo, Teddy Knox, Charlie Naughton, Jimmy Gold and 'Monsewer' Eddie Gray.

Val claimed that he had formed the Crazy Gang in the prewar years and that when Jack reformed them after the war he was stealing another man's creation.

Jack, for his part, maintained that the gang was the work of another great impresario, George Black Senior.

But this did not stop Val insisting that he should have the rights to the name of the comedy team, and detesting Jack for his success with them.

Jack reacted by taking every opportunity to annoy and upset Val and got a great deal of impish pleasure – and profit – whenever he managed to do so.

As the manager of Jack Hylton's television department in the late Fifties I had the job of putting together a six-show 'special' with that tremendous American comic George Jessel, the man who lost the chance of cinema immortality by turning down the Al Jolson role in the world's first talking film 'The Jazz Singer'.

At the time Tommy Trinder was the resident host of 'Sunday Night At The London Palladium', an ATV production and Val's particular baby.

I approached Tommy with the idea of using him in one of the shows with Georgie Jessel as a 'hands across the Atlantic' presentation.

'Nice idea, boy, and I'd love to do it, but I have this exclusive contract for the Sunday Palladium show,' said Tommy.

I asked to see the contract and when I read it I found that the 'exclusivity' applied only to Sundays. During the weekdays Mr Trinder could do what he liked.

Tommy signed for our show and I raced back to tell Jack about it.

The little man was ecstatic with joy. A mile away at his ATV office Val Parnell did not see the funny side of the situation.

Physically, Jack Hylton was not an attractive man – small white-haired and bespectacled. But like many small and successful men he had a terrific, vital charisma... particularly where women were concerned.

He truly loved women and used a large part of his vast

fortune in catering for his romances. He was good to his girl friends and very jealous of them.

One of them he loved most was Pat Marlowe, a petite brunette from the naval town of Chatham, whom he installed in a great style in a beautiful mews house in Mayfair. Pat killed herself in that house with an overdose of drugs in 1962 and Jack never really got over her death. Nor did he ever forget a famous English entertainer who had fathered Pat's only child and then ignored both her and the baby.

The man, who had built his considerable reputation as a 'family' entertainer, was the most despised creature in Jack Hylton's world.

'That bastard will never work for me, not even sweeping the bloody floors,' he vowed. He kept his promise.

Jack's possessiveness over his women could reach almost paranoic lengths. At one time he became convinced that Pat was having an affair with somebody else and was determined to catch her out.

He went to the extravagance of hiring a private detective to 'shadow' Pat and waited in nail-biting agony for a fortnight for the man to produce his report.

The dossier duly arrived... a day by day, almost hourly, log of Pat's excursions and her visitors. One character was constant throughout: an elderly man who had made frequent visits to the mews house in Mount Row.

Hylton seethed as he read it – and then began to match descriptions and the times and dates of the visits.

Pat Marlowe's secret lover was himself!

The detective was upbraided as an idiot, paid off and kicked out. Jack never again stooped to snooping.

One woman at a time was never enough for a man with Jack Hylton's voracious sexual appetite. While he was deeply involved with Pat Marlowe he met an Italian singer (I use the description generously) called Rosalina Neri.

Rosalina was, and is, a woman of great attraction and warmth and a lot of fun to be with, but singing was not her greatest talent.

If Jack had just treated her as a girl friend it would have

been fine, but he was hell-bent on indulging her ambition to sing grand opera... whatever the cost to his pocket and his credibility.

He paid for her singing lessons and put a lot of money into her operatic debut in Italy. The result was a fiasco. Poor Rosalina was roasted by the critics.

She was resilient enough to come through it all still smiling, but Jack felt foolish, something which hurt him deeply.

Ridicule was one thing he could not take, even in its mildest form and some years after I left his office I presented singer Shani Wallis cabaret in London. One of Shani's songs was a parody on 'Personality' which I had specially written for her.

Part of the song ran: 'Rosalina Neri isn't the singer she's cracked up to be – but Jack Hylton knows she's got personality...'

It was harmless enough material, but Jack was in Shani's first night audience, and he was livid.

After the show he sought me out and hissed at me: 'Don't try to get laughs at my expense. Understand?'

The amazing success of the Grades – Lew, Leslie and Bernard Delfont – is one of the great stories in show business. The three brothers from London's East End built the most powerful theatrical agency in Britain.

But I have often wondered if they would have managed it without Warrant Officer Turnbull.

At the beginning of World War Two Leslie Grade was conscripted into the Royal Air Force and with that fine geographical sense that sends Scotsmen to Cornwall and East Anglians to the wilds of Wales, his masters at the Air Ministry decided, through their underlings, that the Cockney airman would be best suited to a posting in the North of England.

Meanwhile, at home in London, Leslie had left his business.

It was here that Warrant Officer Turnbull came on to the scene. Turnbull was one of those indispensable N.C.Os who shuffled people from one air force camp to another from behind the safety of an orderly room desk.

Leslie soon realised the value of this powerful man. A sum of money changed hands and Leslie found himself posted to Ruislip, Middlesex, a camp within easy reach of his home in Streatham, South London, and his West End office in Charing Cross Road.

For nearly two years Charing Cross Road saw more of him than the camp at Ruislip, although he did manage to assuage any ill-feeling that might have arisen among his air force comrades by putting on a couple of shows for them.

But, sadly, there was no Turnbull at Ruislip and someone who was not as sensitive to the demands of British show business, nor as corruptible, posted Leslie to Egypt. A fine place for a Jewish boy!

However, I have no doubt that the work put in by Leslie during his time – or lack of it – at Ruislip was of great importance in the foundation of the Grade empire.

Until now the part played by Turnbull in the fortunes of the Grade brothers has been a secret known to very few, myself included.

I have been privy to it because... the good warrant officer was my first father-in-law!

Leslie was the greatest agent I have ever known, arguably the greatest our business has ever seen. He would promise anything to get what he wanted and then go out on a limb to make sure it materialised.

For a kindly man he had a very ruthless streak and his razor-sharp business sense crippled some people. Not surprisingly he lost friends and one of the most unhappy feuds was that which existed between Leslie and a veteran London agent Joe Collins, the father of film actress Joan and writer Jackie.

Joe had found Dave King as a young comedian and singer and was building him up when Leslie decided to add Dave to his client list.

He got to Dave and offered him all sorts of tempting situations. The promises were hard to reject and Dave signed with him.

From that moment until the time that Leslie died Joe never

spoke to him and his ill-feeling also extended to Leslie's two brothers, Bernard and Lew. In Lew's case it was a specially unhappy situation because in the years before the war he had been in partnership with Joe in an agency called Collins and Grade.

I remember Lew from those days as a little man who ran all over the place. He was never still and never stopped working. It is hardly surprising that he should eventually head the giant Associated Communications Corporation; even though he has now been ousted from his place there.

Lew's profligate investment in the film industry has been blamed for his failure – at the age of 75 – at ACC, but he was always a great chancer.

In 1942 I had an office in Blackpool. I came to London to see Lew at his office in Chandos Place in the West End.

That day he booked every variety act I had on my books – UNSEEN. Actions like that were typical of the man. They showed his horizons and to me it was an acknowledgment of my own standing in the business.

Lew (now Lord Grade) has always believed in the policy of the ever-open door. You never know who might walk through it. Leslie, on the other hand, was a far more distant man. He was hard to get to see and there was always the promise of a return telephone call which never materialised.

I was a director of the Bernard Delfont Agency and its successors, The Grade Organisation and London Management, and worked under the chairmanship of both Leslie and Bernard.

During an office conversation Bernard Delfont told me: 'Never forget that pros are just numbers. That's it: numbers and no more.'

Had I taken that advice to heart I might have saved myself a lot of grief. But I would have missed a lot of good times.

The one member of the Grade family I ever ran foul of was Leslie's son Michael. In a business as dynastic as theirs seemed destined to be it was only natural that when Leslie Grade became too ill to carry on working his place at London Management should be taken by his only son, a former sports reporter with the London Daily Mirror.

Michael became joint managing director of the company with Billy Marsh, one of the great veterans of the business and a life-long colleague of the Grades.

I had joined the London Management board because I asked Bernard Delfont, then its head, for a job. We struck a deal under which I remained more or less autonomous under the 'umbrella' of the company. I was charged a fee every week for my office space and telephones and split any agency commission with the firm.

Shortly after Michael started running the place in double harness with Billy I was offered a deal by M.A.M, the agency which had Tom Jones, Engelbert Humperdinck and Gilbert O'Sullivan under contract. The terms were simple – and attractive:

I joined M.A.M, handed over all my clients, received a quarter of a million pounds and a seat on the board with an appropriate salary.

I turned the deal down to stay with London Management and collected a payment of thirty thousand for doing so.

I have always felt that Michael resented the company having to pay out that sort of money to keep me and his dislike of me increased when I saved actor Clive Dunn from leaving us.

Michael had handled Clive, star of the popular TV series 'Dad's Army', and he would keep Clive waiting for up to an hour before seeing him and at one meeting after office hours with Michael, Billy Marsh and I was told that Clive was leaving the agency.

When I left the meeting I telephoned Clive's home and was told by his wife that he had just left for a holiday alone in Spain. I called my chauffeur and was driven to London's Heathrow airport where I intercepted Clive as he checked in.

For the next five years he was my client. I arranged a recording deal for him under which he made 'Grandad' one of those freak records which went to Number one and stayed in the charts for thirty weeks.

All of this meant more money for London Management

and we had managed to hang on to a valuable client. Michael Grade did not appreciate that and our relationship worsened, although we never had a real confrontation over his feelings towards me.

I first upset Val Parnell when I managed to sign Tommy Trinder to work for Val's old enemy Jack Hylton, but later I was to clash with him in my own right. And it was all over Shirley Bassey.

Leslie Grade wanted Shirley to appear on 'Sunday Night At The London Palladium' and I did not want her to do it because the show did not, at that time, figure in my plans for building her into an international name.

At the same time I did not want to offend Leslie, so I laid down what I thought were conditions that they would never agree to and that way we could all withdraw with honour intact.

'To start with,' I told Leslie, 'I want two thousand five hundred pounds for the date.'

'Done.'

I had not expected this, but now that it had happened I decided to push my luck as far as I could and make an EVENT out of Shirley's TV appearance.

'There are two more conditions, Leslie. Her name is billed alone and bigger than anybody else's and it is surrounded by lights and she does not have to stand on that carousel waving goodbye at the end of the show.'

'I'll have to talk to Val about that,' said Leslie. 'It's very much his show when it comes to things like that.'

Later he called me and told me that Parnell had agreed to my conditions and Shirley and I went ahead to prepare for the show.

At the rehearsal for the show on the Sunday afternoon I learned that there would be no 'Shirley Bassey' in lights and that she would have to take her final bow with everyone else – from the carousel.

I stormed over to Val Parnell, who was sitting watching the run-through from a seat in the red plush stalls.

'This is not what you agreed,' I told him. 'I know that these conditions are not in the contract but Leslie agreed them and a deal's a deal.'

'I don't know what you are talking about,' said Parnell. 'You are getting paid a lot for this show and there'll be no special treatment.'

'Then there will be no Bassey,' I said. 'I am going back to the Dorchester Hotel with her and when you keep your word we will come back and do the show.'

Back at the hotel we waited until seven p.m, an hour before the show was due to start, before Leslie Grade telephoned.

'Val has been giving me hell,' he said. 'Can't you just leave things as they are?'

'No deal Leslie. Her name in lights and a solo exit. They were terms.'

The next voice I heard was Val Parnell's.

'We are doing what you want, Sullivan. Now get that bloody girl over here!'

And that's how Shirley Bassey became the only star not to appear on that famous Palladium merry-go-round. That is if you don't count the time that Dave King stopped it completely.

ACT THREE
Scene One: The Girl From Tiger Bay

She was sitting on the dusty floor of a bare rehearsal studio. Old, crumpled jeans were rolled to her knees and a pale tan face with a short-cropped fuzz of black hair topped a dirty yellow sweater.

Just looking at the girl made me half decide to send her away and find somebody else. But everybody deserves a chance and I had paid her train fare from Wales to London. I said:

'Well, I guess we had better hear this young lady sing.'

The girl on the floor was Shirley Bassey, then just eighteen years old and totally unknown. Before long I was to guide and groom her to becoming the most popular female singer in the world.

Looking back, I think that at the time of our first meeting – at Max Rivers rehearsal rooms in Great Newport Street, just off London's Charing Cross Road, on February 14, 1955 – I must have been out of mind.

For Shirley Bassey still, in my sleepless nights, haunts me.

But a little madness is good for all of us...

Maybe I was sub-consciously looking for a new horizon at the time, for I seemed to have been doing it all wrong up to then.

After eleven years building up my own theatrical agency, Michael Sullivan Limited, I controlled the booking of twenty three variety theatres and had seventy two acts on my books. I also produced my own touring shows, revues, pantomimes and ice spectaculars.

It should have been good except theatres were closing all

over the country, shows were playing to empty houses and there was no work for my acts.

Britain had discovered television and people were using my box office money to pay the instalments on their sets.

One theatre group went bust owing me two thousand pounds and I was in debt myself.

I still had enough enthusiasm to grab the telephone whenever it rang and one morning towards the end of January that year I took a call from John Marriner, controller of the Little Theatre in Jersey, in the Channel Islands. John asked if I could book him a small ballet company and I suggested the Ben Johnson Dancers, a skilful all-Negro group. He agreed and asked me to book them for him.

When I went to see the group rehearse it occured to me that, as he was going to do a complete show on Jersey, Ben would need an act to keep the show together in front of the stage curtain while he changed his sets. A singer might be the answer I told Ben. Did he know anybody?

'How about Shirley Bassey?' chipped in one of his girls while Johnson was thinking of names.

'Who's Shirley Bassey?' I said. You can ask a simple question like that without knowing what you are getting into. After all, somebody must have said one day 'I wonder how you split an atom?'...

Shirley Bassey, I learned, had been a singer in two shows 'Memories Of Jolson' and 'Hot From Harlem' in which the Johnson dancers had toured.

'Any good?' I asked.

'Not bad,' said one of the dancers. 'But I'm not sure if she is still in the business.'

Ben Johnson said the girl lived in Cardiff and offered to get in touch with her. In the event of her wanting to audition, he gave me her address:

Shirley Bassey, 132 Partmanmoor Road, Splott, Cardiff.

Splott! So this is what our glittering business has come to, I thought, and went for a drink.

The girl replied and I sent her the train fare. A few minutes before six p.m. on February 14 I climbed two flights of bare wooden stairs to the rehearsal room.

A pianist called Stanley Myers was sitting at an upright piano, waiting. I walked over to the girl on the floor and Ben Johnson introduced us. She grinned an urchin grin and held out a dust-grimed hand. She didn't bother to get up.

When we had met she stood up and walked over to the piano. I tried to ease the strain of the audition by asking her: 'In the last shows you did... was there any song that you were specially comfortable with?'

She said: 'Yes, I'd like to sing "Stormy Weather".'

She had no idea of what key she wanted, but she sang a few soft bars and the patient Stanley Myers sorted out the right chords.

'Well, do you think you're set?' I asked.

'I'll do my best.'

She said this very humbly. I was later to learn that with Shirley Bassey this was one of life's rare moments.

When she did sing I could see no more than her face peeping over the top of the piano. With her loud and powerful voice she reached out for the high notes and hit them... clear and true.

As she did it I shivered, an uncanny spine-tingling sensation. This had never happened to me before and I was hardened to singers and their auditions.

I told Ben the girl would be suitable and left him to fix the terms with her. Later Johnson, his wife, one of his dancers named Louise and the scruffy girl singer joined me for a drink.

Shirley drank lemonade in the nearby pub and I asked her if she had ever auditioned for a recording company.

'People have said they would fix it up, but they never did,' she replied. I told her that I expected to be going to Jersey during the summer season. 'We'll have a cup of tea and talk about it.'

'That will be nice.' She sounded as if she didn't believe a word of it.

I walked the few yards to the Mapleton Hotel in Coventry Street. I had not thought of going to Jersey. Why had I told this kid I would.

I was living at the hotel with my wife Juhni, and all through the night I kept talking about this girl and her voice.

On the Monday the show was due to open at the Little Theatre I caught a plane to Jersey and sat through the matinee performance listening to Shirley Bassey sing 'Stormy Weather', 'Ebb Tide', 'Smile' and 'The Sunny Side Of The Street'.

She looked terrible in a pale green, calf-length dress she had bought for her sister's wedding and with no sense of make-up.

None of this made any difference. It could all be changed. What mattered was that I still got that shiver when she sang.

All of the Svengali that lives in every real agent was getting to work within me. I would mould her, teach her stage-craft, lighting, build her into a star.

Because she was coloured it would be easy to persuade people to think of her, properly presented, like Lena Horne or Eartha Kitt. I was being sucked into a vortex of dreams, but I still needed some moral support to boost my hunch.

After the audition I had asked Stanley Myers what he thought of the girl. 'She sings a song,' he said dismissively.

From Jersey I telephoned an old friend on neighbouring Guernsey, Sydney James, booker for that island's Cany Gardens Theatre. He came to Jersey, listened to all my enthusiasm and sat in the circle of the theatre to listen to Shirley sing her first two songs.

The audience applauded loudly, but Sydney was unimpressed. 'I think you are out of your mind, Sullivan,' he said.

'Sydney you are so wrong. Look at the audience. This kid's got them eating out of her hand. Wait until I dress her up, teach her to move, get her made up properly, get her some special numbers. Use your imagination.'

'My knowledge and experience are what I use,' he said. 'She sings out of tune and you can forget the audience. Audiences are like sheep. One claps, they all follow. You have got to get her past the bookers before the public will see her and no booker is going to go for her.'

It made no difference. Sydney had failed to back my

judgment, but I was convinced I was right.

After the show Sydney and I gathered in the lounge of the hotel with Ben Johnson and his wife, Shirley and the dancer Louise. Physically I had been attracted to Louise from the time I first saw her in that rehearsal room and if she had been able to sing – just a little – I would never have asked Ben to send that telegram to Cardiff.

I arranged things so that Shirley and I would sit away from the rest. When we were alone I sat and listened as she, reluctantly at first, told me the story of her life.

'I was born,' she said, 'in Bute Road, in Tiger Bay, the Cardiff dock area. My mother is a Yorkshire woman and my father is a West African seaman. I haven't seen him since I was two. There are seven children. I'm the youngest.'

She left school at fifteen and went to work wrapping enamel basins in a factory. On Saturday evenings she sang in pubs and working men's clubs with a trio for one pound a time.

A Welsh producer who was putting on an all-Negro show 'Memories Of Jolson' saw her in a pub and asked her to go to London for an audition. She got the job and toured for five months at ten pounds a week.

'I wasn't sure I liked it,' she said. 'I enjoyed the singing, but not the travelling, not living in digs. And I didn't get on too well with some of the people in the show.'

After that tour she appeared for six months – at fourteen pounds a week this time – in another Negro show 'Hot From Harlem'. That tour ended and she got no more offers.

'I got a job as a waitress in a little cafe in Cardiff. I was working there when you sent for me,' she finished.

I waited a few moments and then asked: 'How would you like to go out on your own, on a variety tour.'

'On my own. Oh, I don't think I would like that.'

'Well, not exactly on your own. You would have a pianist and I would be with you.'

She said nothing.

'You see,' I said, 'I believe that if you will work with me I can make you into a star.'

Her response was to burst into soft, silent tears. She had been told things like this before and nothing had happened. She was eighteen and disillusioned.

I got up and held my hand out to her. 'It's time you were in bed,' I said. 'I'm going back to London tomorrow. Come to see me as soon as this job is over and we'll see what we can work out.'

She nodded and smiled through the tears.

Moments like that I cannot resist. I kept hold of her hand and lead her upstairs to bed with me.

That was the first and only time I made love to Shirley Bassey. Had I done it more often everything might have been different. We might still be together today. But that night showed me a side to her that was surprising.

That doubting, insecure girl from Tiger Bay was a tigress in her own right. My back was so badly mauled and scratched by her that the following day I telephoned my office and my wife saying that I had to stay on in the Channel Islands.

Then I went to Guernsey for five days to let the scars heal.

After my return to London I waited for Ben Johnson's group to finish in Jersey, then every day when I walked into the office I asked my secretary: 'Did a coloured girl call today? Someone called Bassey?'

She had not called and she did not call. After more than a week I started chasing her. Nobody knew where she was... most of the people I telephoned had never heard of her anyway.

One afternoon I rang Max Rivers' rehearsal rooms and found Ben Johnson there. He said he would get a message to her. I asked him to tell her to come to my office at five p.m. the following Saturday.

She came. At the time I was lying in bed in the Mapleton Hotel, streaming eyes and a high temperature, a victim to 'flu. Juhni, my wife, had to go to the office and meet her on the street. She missed her, but once again I tracked her down to the rehearsal rooms and told her to come to the hotel.

She walked through the door half an hour later wearing a

transparent raincoat over a salmon-pink dress. Juhni was not impressed.

When I had introduced her to Juhni I began to talk, saying I was sure I could build her into a star if she would do what she was told.

The girl seemed doubtful until I said: 'Let's put it this way: Would you enter into a contract with me under which I guaranteed you a certain amount each week whether you work or not, for at least a year?'

'What do you mean by a certain amount?'

'We would have to work this out, but it would probably be about twenty pounds a week.'

She looked puzzled. Juhni, in the meantime, looked horrified – she knew the financial state of Michael Sullivan Limited.

'How can you pay me that much if I don't work?'

'You'll be working, rehearsing about four hours a day. I'm prepared to invest in you and if we both work hard I'll get it all back and more.'

Juhni looked imploringly at the ceiling as though divine providence might at any moment intervene and bring this farce to an end.

'It's a gamble,' I said. 'And you can't lose.'

'Oh, all right then,' Shirley said. I blew my nose and a star was born.

'I'll draw up a contract which will guarantee you a fixed wage every week. I'll pay for your stage costumes, music, a pianist, publicity, your rehearsal rooms, travelling and commission to agents.

'Now go away and talk it over with your mother and your friends. When you're happy call me.'

Shirley got up to leave.

'You'll see,' I said as she went through the door, 'You'll be up there with Lena Horne in a couple of years.'

'Goodbye Mr Sullivan,' she said shyly.

Now it was Juhni's turn. 'I just hope you know what you are doing,' she said, 'She's not bad looking, but she's no raving beauty. She'll need a lot of working on just to give her presence.'

Juhni came from an old show business family (her uncle was Jimmy Nervo of the Crazy Gang), she was a top West End stage costume designer and she knew the business. But she had not heard Shirley sing.

'Wait until you hear her sing,' I said.

I still needed somebody, anybody, to confirm my faith in the girl. I went to see two veterans in the variety business, Joe Collins and Sydney Burns. We talked about this girl called Shirley Bassey. What did they think?

Joe, who had managed 'Hot From Harlem', told me: 'She walked out of the show before the end.'

Sydney had a share in her first show 'Memories of Jolson'. His judgment: 'She is still a beginner. A baby. She sang out of tune and she shouted more than she sang. She's not much.'

Back with Juhni, I said: 'I had a word with Joe Collins and Sydney Burns about Shirley.'

'And?'

'They said she's great. Said it was time somebody did something about it,' I lied.

When Shirley came to this office the next time I had a draft contract ready for her. It ran for six months and after that I had the option to carry on with new clauses for five years.

I sent her back to Cardiff to show it to her mother. I needed her mother's signature to make it legal. The girl was still only eighteen years old and, in law, a minor.

A few days later she returned. The contract had been approved by her mother and she was ready to sign.

'By the way,' I said. 'You're sure you don't have a contract with anybody else?'

'No,' she said. 'I did have one with an agency. My Mam signed it. But it's been cancelled.'

'What do you mean – cancelled?'

She looked uneasy and I told her:

'Shirley. You are holding out on me. You didn't tell me that you left "Hot From Harlem" before the run ended, but I found that out. What else don't I know?'

Then she told all . . . or very nearly all. She had left the show to have a baby and after her daughter was born and she was ready to work again her agents offered her nothing. The baby was being taken care of by her married sister and she took the job as a waitress. As far as she was concerned her deal with the agency was over.

'But you're not married?'
'No.'
'So where's the father?'   'I haven't seen him since.'
'Will you tell me who he is?'
'No.'

Before we got down to making her a star Shirley and I decided right then on a cover-up operation over the baby, Sharon.

'If you do become famous this is the sort of stuff certain newspapers will make a meal of,' I explained. In those days illegitimacy was not treated with the tolerance it is today.

We agreed, that apart from her family, the baby would be our secret.

'Now you know,' she said sadly, 'I don't suppose you think very much of me, do you?'

'Dear girl,' I said, 'How can I think anything? I'm a bastard myself!'

She signed the contract and Svengali Sullivan got to work. Late at night we would sit in my office in Shaftesbury Avenue discussing the timing and phrasing of songs. I made her speak the words until she was able to break up a lyric and make every syllable count.

Shirley and a pianist called Bon Wardlaw worked together for four hours a day for three months until she developed a style of her own.

Juhni advised on costumes and to make Shirley look old enough for the sophisticated songs she was singing I decided she should wear black velvet with elbow length gloves and a false hairpiece to give her height.

She hated the dress and swore she would never wear it. She did.

I taught her how to act out her songs and made her practise that most difficult part of stage craft – walking off. Anyone can get on a stage... getting off is a different story, and until she learned how to do it precisely I would end her act by lowering the curtains while she still faced the audience.

Then she learned how to make contact with every member of the audience, just by looking.

'After the first sixteen bars of a song their attention begins to wander,' I said. 'Until then they are busy taking you in. That's when you have to get them and hold them. Take them one side at a time and let your eyes go from the front to the middle, to the back.

'You don't have to move much and when you get a high note throw your head back and give it to the people upstairs. That way you get all of them and keep them.'

From my limited resources I was investing heavily in her. Bob Wardlaw cost me twelve pounds a week and the rehearsal rooms came to a pound a day. Shirley got ten pounds a week and the occasional pound for a cinema visit to indulge her addiction to science fiction films.

Her testing time came at the Hippodrome Theatre, Keighley in Yorkshire. I was asked to book a variety bill for the Hippodrome and placed Shirley in the second top position. It was the first time she appeared as a solo act on any stage.

That second top billing worried her. I had not told her that I was booking the show. I wanted her to think that somebody had asked for her. 'It's the best thing that could happen,' I explained. 'We have got to hit it hard. Nothing in your career must look as though you are creeping into the business. We start at the top – or as near to it as we can get.'

Keighley... the top?

Bob Wardlaw and I saw Shirley through the Monday morning band call and two afternoon dress rehearsals. By the time it came for Shirley to go on stage and close the first half of the show she was near to panic.

At the back of the stage I stood with her, rubbing her numb, cold hands, trying to stop her shivering. 'Don't worry. Just go out and sing. It doesn't matter if you make mistakes. Just try to do everything we have worked at all these weeks,' I said.

As the pit orchestra played 'I Can't Give You Anything

But Love' I pushed her gently forward and then ran through the door from the stage area into the auditorium.

She had already finished her first song when I got round there and the applause sounded good. After her second number it was much louder.

I stopped watching Shirley to take in the audience. There were about sixty old people among the Monday nighters - traditionally made up of a lot of complimentary and half price tickets.

It was the old people I watched. They were applauding as keenly as anybody in that theatre. For me that was all the confirmation I needed of my faith in Shirley Bassey.

'These are the very last people her act is aimed at and yet she had got them,' I thought. 'The girl really has something.'

By the end of that week at Keighley Shirley was stopping the show with 'Stormy Weather' and even the taciturn Yorkshire manager at the Hippodrome had to admit: 'I've heard better, you know, but I must say she goes over bloody well.'

She did not work in a theatre for the next two weeks. I used the time to change some of her songs and make changes in the stage lighting for her act.

She then went on an eleven week tour of provincial theatres. In nine towns she was well received, by the audiences and the local critics. But at Northampton where she appeared in New Theatre I had reports from the manager that she had 'died' and my old Guernsey friend Sydney James rang me on her opening night at his theatre and told me:

'They hated her. She's terrible. I'm thinking of paying her off.' He ranted at me for so long that I just stopped listening and put the telephone under a cushion.

The next morning I called him.

'What are we going to do about it?'

'I've done it,' said Sydney. 'I've cut her act from twenty five minutes to eight minutes.'

I was thunderstruck, but he was the boss in his own theatre and there was nothing I could do. There is no complete explanation for Shirley's bad performances, but those two reactions made me think: Was I wasting my time?

The other worry I had was that I was losing money. I had expected this, but I had not been prepared for just how much. I was being paid thirty five pounds a week for Shirley's services. Out of this I paid twelve pounds to her pianist and eighteen to Shirley. I paid their fares, three pounds ten shillings agent's commission, bought music and paid for publicity photographs.

In addition to this I became aware that my girl had a very suspicious mind and to make it clear to her that I was not exploiting her I asked her to collect her cheque at the end of the week, take out her salary and send the rest to me.

For a while this arrangement worked and then she stopped sending me my share. After a month without money and bills to pay on her behalf I wrote her an angry letter demanding that she came to my office on a Monday after she had finished a week in the Cumberland town of Workington.

When she arrived it was all too obvious that the change I had hoped for was already taking place in that shy little girl from Cardiff. She stalked about the office and arrogantly told me:

'This is my money. I pay you.'

'No Shirley. You don't pay me. I pay you. I'm promoting you.'

'I wanted an association where we worked as a team. With any luck both of us might be earning big money a few years from now, but I'm wondering if you are worth bothering about.'

I thought for a moment and then came to a decision that – had I followed through with it – would have changed both our lives.

I decided to kick her out.

'It doesn't look as if you are the sort of person who can work in this way. Let's forget the whole thing.'

She began to cry.

The tears were genuine, but I had already seen a side of Miss Bassey that I didn't like... the haughty, demanding egotistical side... and I decided to relent but let her sweat for a while.

'I've got a lot of work to do now. The best thing you can do is go away and think things over. You may come back tomorrow and we'll see whether it is worth going on.'

Head drooping, she walked to the door. The next day she telephoned and asked meekly: 'Am I to come in today?'

I pretended to take time to think about my work load. 'Make it five o'clock,' I ordered.

When she arrived I asked her in my best head teacher style: 'How do you feel about it now?'

'I'd like to straighten things out,' she said. 'And let's go on. Please, Mr Sullivan.'

MISTER Sullivan. That's the sort of attitude I wanted.

'Willingly, Shirley,' I said, stern but forgiving. 'Now tell me why you didn't send me the money.'

The answer was simple. She had been sued for back commission by her previous agents. It amounted to only forty pounds or so and I arranged to pay it off and collect it from her in instalments.

I now had time to concentrate on her future career. That year the record business was fantastic. Records were making stars who had never been seen on a stage or on TV.

But Shirley had a visual personality as well as a voice so I decided to keep her away from records and let her make her name in live performance.

But where? Keighley? Northampton? Workington? She could do... in about thirty years.

Piece by piece I put my mental jigsaw together: A coloured girl, sexy looking, singing sophisticated, moody songs. Like Lena Horne, like Eartha Kitt, like Josephine Baker.

In the bottom of my glass I saw images of them performing. Around them were audiences sitting at tables. I had found the answer:

Cabaret.

I went to see Bertie Green.

Bertie ran the Astor Club, a gilded cavern at the south end of Berkeley Square where a lot of newcomers had been given their chance.

I gave him all the sales talk about this girl who was different and sensational and was just what he had been looking for all these years. Then I got Sonny Zahl, another agent to make a deal with him. I was already becoming a bit of joke in the business with my dedication to an unknown that I felt it would be better if an independent agent sold her.

Sonny got Shirley sixty five pounds a week for a two-week engagement and then I had to produce something to live up to everything I had told Bertie.

In the years I watched international stars in cabaret I had noticed one thing – they all had material specially written for them. I wanted a song, her own song, just for Shirley.

Benny Lee, the singer, comedian and disc jockey, used to lunch frequently at the Universal Chinese restaurant in Denmark Street, London's 'Tin Pan Alley'. Another regular was Ross Taylor, the man who wrote 'The Girl In The Alice Blue Gown' and 'There'll Always Be An England'.

'Introduce me,' I said to Benny, but he had never heard Shirley sing and was reticent about denting his friendship with Parker.

'I would want to see her first.'

That week, just to do me a favour, he travelled to Chatham in Kent where Shirley was appearing. She impressed him enough to say:

'She's a rough diamond, but it's worth letting Ross take a look.'

I met Ross and he, too, agreed to visit Chatham. After the show we drove back to London.

'Yes,' said Ross, 'I'm prepared to write a couple of songs for the girl, but I suppose you know how much I get?'

'I've no idea. You'll have to tell me. I've never bought a song.'

'I usually get in the neighbourhood of two hundred guineas.'

This was about one hundred and seventy five pounds more than I could handle, but I said: 'That seems a fair price' and we arranged to meet at my mother-in-law's flat, where there was a piano, and discuss songs.

In that flat Ross played and sang his own songs for four hours. I was so impressed that I wanted to manage him as a singer, but none of the songs he had sung seemed right for Shirley. Politely I explained this and he said: 'What the hell do you want?'

'I want some bite in the lines, something saucy. I want her to sell sex.'

We talked around this and talked of the people we wanted to interest, the international night club set... the people who burnt the candle at both ends. At last we had the idea, and Ross said:

'I'll go away and work on it.'

The song he produced was banned by the coy British Broadcasting Corporation the moment they heard it, but when he handed 'Burn My Candle' over to me I knew that it was what I had been looking for.

At that meeting I asked him: 'What do you really think of Shirley?'

'I really think,' he said, 'that you have got something there.'

He liked her. That helped me push home my next point:

'I have always felt that about her and I'm putting everything I've got behind her. I hope it is going to pay off big. But right now I'm losing money on her.'

I gave this time to sink in and went on:

'The trouble is, Ross, I need this song badly but I can't pay you for it.'

'What do you mean – nothing?'

'I'm glad you mentioned that figure, because that's it. Nothing.'

I waited a moment before following up with: 'The truth is, I can't afford to hand out two hundred guineas, but if you would like to make a price I'd be glad to buy it on the instalment plan.'

At first this big amiable man looked startled, then amused. He looked at me and said: 'I rather like you. I'll help you all I can.'

He sold me 'Burn My Candle' for one hundred and fifty pounds at fifteen pounds a week for ten weeks. The song that launched Shirley Bassey to international stardom was bought on the never-never!

I decided to push my luck.

'I need a lot more help yet, Ross.'

'Oh. In what way?'

'Would you go to Hull, to the Tivoli Theatre there, and play music for Shirley for the week before she goes into the Astor? I want you to play in the show every night and rehearse her in this one song every morning.'

'I shall need,' he said, 'a vast amount of money for all this.'

'All of twenty five pounds a week?'

He pulled a diary from his pocket, studied it and then looked up. 'I'll have to get out of a couple of things that week. Is that really the most you can afford?'

I showed him how, after paying Shirley eighteen pounds, him twenty five and the agent's commission I was already money out on the thirty five pounds a week she was getting at Hull, and I still had not paid fares, publicity expenses and incidentals.

'The only way for me to make a profit out of it is to drop the whole thing.'

Ross could do his arithmetic too. 'Okay,' he said. 'Twenty five it is.'

Half-way through his week at Hull with Shirley he telephoned me and asked: 'Who's playing for her at the Astor?'

I was going to rely on the band.

'You can't do that,' said Ross. 'You'll have to have me.'

'How much.'

'Seeing as it's you Mike, I'll do it for the same money. Twenty five a week.'

When I heard Ross Parker take Shirley through that song in rehearsal I knew that everything I had ever felt about her was right. I celebrated by buying her a new dress for the Astor – white, tight down to the knees, then flaring to the floor. She looked fantastic.

Shirley's first show at the Astor was at one in the morning. The audience were screaming and shouting by the time she got to 'Burn My Candle'. When she sang the song the place broke up.

Every night she got better and better. Every night I hugged her and myself – and anybody else who happened to be around – with delight.

Then, on the Wednesday of her second week there, Ross who had given her such terrific coaching and backing, called me at my hotel room. 'I hear Jack Hylton's coming tonight,' he said. 'Be there.'

That night at the Astor I watched the famous little showman walk in with Robert Dhery, the French comedian and producer. I thought at the time that he had come to see Shirley after a call from Ross who had written scores for Hylton shows. The truth was that he was there simply because Dhery had wanted to go. Shirley Bassey wasn't even a consideration.

At midnight Ross came into the club, walked to my table and said: 'Come and meet Jack.'

At Hylton's table the great man talked to me, not about Shirley but about television. He wanted to hear my views of TV light entertainment and how to organise an office to deal with shows for TV.

He stopped talking when Shirley started singing. After the tumultous applause that had become the expected during the previous nine days he looked round at me and said: 'She's very good, you know.

'Do you think she could open at the Adelphi tomorrow night?'

I tried to be blasé: 'I think it could be possible.'

'I'll tell you,' he said in his quiet Lancastrian voice. 'This girl I've got, Pavlou, she's been taken off with peritonitis and I've got to find somebody to fill a small spot. You know lad, it's only a little time, not important to the show, but we need some girl and this one's not bad.'

Marie Pavlou, the Greek singer who was in the Adelphi show was ill and Shirley had her chance.

Then came the second surprise of the night.

'Now how about yourself,' said Hylton. 'What about you coming to work for me?'

I did not quite understand.

'You see,' he added, 'I'm setting up a television department and I think you could run it. Would you like it?'

'It's late,' I said. 'My first thought is yes, I would, but I have a going business. How soon would you need me?'

'Oh, almost immediately. Come and see me at ten tomorrow and we'll decide if your girl should go into the Adelphi and then we'll have lunch and talk about you.'

At ten in the morning I was at his office in Saville Row. Overnight I had made up my mind about my future. If the offer was good enough I would wind up my business and take it.

But first on the agenda was Shirley.

'Yes,' said Hylton, 'I want the girl for the Adelphi. You'll need to sort out which numbers she'll sing and fix the band parts.'

We settled on four songs, including 'Burn My Candle' but as it had never been published there was no band music for it. We did not even have a score for a pianist.

I tracked Ross down to Brighton, telephoned him and he sang the melody line of the song to Billy Ternant, the orchestra conductor at the Adelphi. Billy noted it down and then scored it for the band.

While all this went on I was agreeing to go to work for Jack Hylton myself for one thousand five hundred pounds for the first year, two thousand for the second and two thousand five hundred for the third with five pounds a week expenses and a twenty five per cent interest in his agency, Jack Hylton Limited.

In return my agency was merged with his.

After selling us both to Hylton I telephoned Shirley at Olivelli's, an Italian restaurant off London's Tottenham Court Road where rooms above were rented to theatricals.

She was not fully awake when I told her: 'Get yourself ready and go straight to the Adelphi Theatre. You have to rehearse because you're going on tonight.'

'Pull the other leg.'

I bellowed: 'Leave the funny lines to the comic. You just have to sing. Get moving. I'll see you there.'

The curtain went up on the first show at the Adelphi at six fifteen p.m. At least it did on every other night. This evening Shirley and the band were still running through 'Burn My Candle' and then they had to rehearse 'Stormy Weather'. While they did the ticket holders were jamming the foyer, wondering why the doors were still locked.

I used all my persuasion on a panic-stricken house manager to hold them off for another fifteen minutes to give Shirley time to finish her rehearsal and then went to see comedian Dave King who was the star of the show.

I knew Dave would have to introduce Shirley and wanted to be sure it would be done well.

'What's her name?' he asked.

'Shirley Bassey.'

'Don't worry, I'll give her a build-up. It will be fine.'

The show started and a few minutes before Shirley's spot I was standing in the wings. Dave was there, waiting to make his entrance. He turned to me:

'That girl's name was what?'

'Shirley Bassey. Shir-ley Bass ... look Dave, it's too risky. I'll write it down for you.'

I wrote it down and he went on. At the end of his routine I was standing backstage with Shirley and listened as he gave her a superb introduction finishing with: 'So it is my great pleasure to introduce – Shirley ...'

He had forgotten the name.

Happily Shirley was too excited to notice. She went out and assaulted that audience and performed like a demon.

Three newspapermen who had been invited by the show's publicist George Fearon to come in to see the new singer rushed to Shirley's dressing room. Fearon made more calls to tell others who had been invited but had better things to do what they were missing. A few more turned up for the second performance and afterward a dazed Shirley was photographed in a gold sheath dress Jack Hylton had got out of store for her.

She had to remember not to turn round. The dress was pinned at the back so it would fit.

The following morning Shirley Bassey appeared in the national newspapers for the first time. I wanted to share her excitement, but left it until noon before I telephoned her.

'Have you seen the papers?'

'What papers? Leave me alone. I want to go back to sleep.'

At that moment I could have killed her...

Scene Two: Shirley's Ascending Star

The danger signs were all around. Newspapers were hailing Shirley as 'Jack Hylton's newest discovery' and Jack was asking for a share in my contract with her to go along with the agency clients I had already merged with his company.

I stalled – mainly because I had no permanent deal with Shirley and also because I did not feel like sharing my creation with anybody.

Shirley had only a few days left at the Adelphi. In fact she was deputising for a deputy, comedian Tony Hancock who had originally stood in for Maria Pavlou. Tony was due back after the week-end.

On the Saturday evening I brought Shirley's mother and sisters from Cardiff to London. After seeing the show they made a nice family group in the dressing room for pictures of Shirley signing a five year contract with me.

This guaranteed her twenty five pounds a week for the first year and sixty pounds a week for the second. From then on we had a partnership: I got forty five per cent of all income and paid for gowns, publicity, music, pianists and travel. She got the rest.

At the time the deal meant only one thing to me – I was losing even more money. Because of her small success at the Adelphi, Shirley's price went up to about sixty pounds a week, but every day I had to pay out for entertaining people who were interviewing her; publicity material; fan photographs... and the Bassey side of my personal ledger was heavily in the red.

One night Shirley appeared in a Jack Hylton TV and, as a result, I signed her to a recording contract with Philips

Records. Her first record sold well but it was no block-busting success.

It was obvious that I could not push Shirley as a teen-age idol. The songs she sang and her entire presentation were against it. Her recording manager, Johnny Franz, agreed with me and saw sense in my plan to take her slowly to the top and keep her there.

The next thing I needed for Shirley was a decent run in a West End show. It would keep her in the eye of the top circle in show business . . . and it would also mean that I would have no travelling expense, no gowns and no pianist to pay for.

Jack Hylton was setting up a new Adelphi show and during a taxi ride through the West End one day I said to him: 'The Adelphi show is getting close, Jack. Are you going to use Shirley?'

He shifted deeper into his collar, looked round at me and replied: 'Certainly. We just have to settle terms. Now, what do you think would be fair?'

I knew that if I asked too much Shirley would be out of the show, but – at the same time – I was Jack's employee and owed him a certain loyalty. There was the added complication that in the small print of our contract was a clause which said that in the event of my deal being terminated with his office any artist I brought into the firm was automatically under contract to Jack.

This did not include Shirley, but in every other respect I was Jack Hylton's employee.

Having worked for him for some time I knew the sort of money he paid and asked for seventy five pounds a week, which was too much – but not that much too much. We settled on sixty five pounds. On such flimsy financial foundations stars are built.

The show 'Such Is Life', with comedian Al Read at the top of the bill, opened on December 14, 1955 . . . and Shirley stole nearly all the critical praise.

One critic wrote: 'She sang her songs in a way that amounted to vocal arson. She was all electric and uninsulated. She is an eighteen-year-old coloured girl from the docks in

Cardiff who hit rain-soaked London like a freak heat-wave.'

And: 'On the whole this is a revue for the charabanc trade. Except that Miss Bassey, as she is in the limousine class. But go and see her even if your normal means of transport is by rickshaw, roller skates or drosky.'

I fought for bigger billing for Shirley, but Jack Hylton would not agree – so I gave up, content that life would be a little less hectic once she had settled in for a long run in a theatre just half a mile from her home at Olivelli's.

I had reckoned without Shirley's taste – and appetite – for boy friends.

A lot of men took her seriously when she sang 'Burn My Candle'... and when they chanced their arms they found she was ready for ignition.

Every night she was out on dates after the show with a man and I thought that because she was entitled to a private life it was best not to interfere.

That attitude was fine until I was stopped in a back-stage corridor of the Adelphi by Shirley's dresser, Helen Cooper.

'Mike,' she said, 'I must have a word with you. You have got to talk to Shirley. Her mouth is bruised and it's all because of some boy. She won't tell me about it, maybe you can get it out of her.'

I crashed into Shirley's dressing room and found her dabbing make-up over a swollen lip and jaw. There was also a small cut on her arm.

The start of the show was still an hour away and for most of that hour I shot questions at her. She simply turned away and refused to answer me.

Eventually I broke her down and she told me that she had, indeed, been burning her candle both ends with casual boy friends... and in the middle with a nineteen-year-old who, for months, had considered himself her steady date.

She had stood him up so many times for other men that he had flared up and threatened to beat her up if she went out with anybody else.

The previous night she had gone out with another casual 'pick up' and when she got home to Olivelli's her angry 'steady' was waiting for her.

He pushed her into her room and – amid a lot of shouting – punched her in the face.

'Do something, please do something. I never thought it would get like this,' she begged.

'Shirley,' I asked. 'Do you want to see him again?'

'Oh no, never, never again. Just do something.'

The next morning, furnished with the boy's name and telephone number by Shirley, I called his mother and told her I intended reporting the assault to the police.

His mother was, naturally enough, opposed to this and told me: 'I don't want my boy going out with her. I'll talk to him.'

We agreed that I wouldn't press any charges against the boy, but I said: 'I don't want a court hearing and the publicity it would bring at this stage in Shirley's career.

'But, on the other hand, I can't take the risk of Shirley being injured whenever your boy feels she has done something to deserve it. I just want to persuade a policeman to have a word with him. It can all be done confidentially... and then I suggest we all forget about it.'

After I had called at Bow Street police station and a friendly detective had had a word or two with the boy I thought the matter was over. That was my second mistake.

Within two months Shirley was seeing her slap-happy boy friend again.

They were dating regularly and I could foresee even more trouble on the way. I appealed to Shirley to end the affair, but it was obviously going too well for her to consider that.

'Everything's all right now,' she assured me happily. 'He's never spiteful the way he used to be and I'm quite happy.'

I hoped that the punishing work schedule I was putting her through would kill any daft romantic ideas she had. She was working to the limit... TV appearances, a weekly radio show, opening shops, recording, publicity interviews and picture sessions. She even had two evening jobs at the same time.

While she was still appearing at the Adelphi I contracted for her to sing in cabaret at the Embassy Club in Bond Street. She did two shows a night at the Adelphi and two hours later was singing at the club.

I was beginning to get a return on my investment, and starting to think of Shirley as just a puppet. I forgot that she was a human being and a very emotional one.

One night at the Adelphi she told me how she had fainted at the end of her act. 'But the audience didn't notice, Mr Sullivan. I held out until I got into the wings and fainted there.'

All I said was: 'Next time you feel like fainting do it right there in the middle of the stage. Think of the publicity, girl.'

I realised that I had hurt her and later I sent her flowers to soften the blow. But I could not resist writing on the card that went with them: 'Next time – in the middle of the stage'.

As the work and the publicity increased I began to sense that the uncertain little girl from Cardiff was changing. That star temperament that has since become a vital part of the Bassey personality was showing.

I had arranged for Shirley to appear live on a Friday night TV show between her last show at the Adelphi and her cabaret stint at the Embassy. I called at the theatre to pick her up.

I waited in her dressing room and seconds after the show ended she stormed in, flung part of her costume into the corner and burst into tears.

As I calmed her down she told me that she had argued with the stage director over being in place on time for the finale. She called him names. He retaliated... and then slapped her face.

'But I gave him one whack,' she growled. 'He knew what hit him.' The tears had given way to her anger and she wanted more revenge. Instead I called the stage director in and very diplomatically got the pair of them to shake hands and promise to forget the incident.

'Hurry up and change now, Shirley,' I said. 'We'll have to rush to do this TV on time.'

My puppet gave a dismissive wave of the arm and said in her best Greta Garbo fashion: 'I can't work tonight.'

'Don't be ridiculous. You're billed to appear and it's no use arguing. We have ten minutes.' Then I signalled Helen

Cooper, her dresser, to help her change.

Shirley pushed Helen away and started to rage and stamp.

'I'm not going. I'm not going on television. I'm not well. I'm ill, I tell you, ill!'

She started throwing clothes and pots of make up at me and screaming. Here was the Bassey I was to come to know and shudder over. Screaming and temperamental.

The more I tried to calm her the more hysterical she became. I reacted in the same way as that stage director had. I slapped her in the face.

Maybe I felt guilty about doing it, for I did not put enough sincerity into it and Shirley got worse. She made so much noise that the theatre manager, Bill Porter, heard it.

Bill came into the room and, probably because he was less involved than Helen and I, he managed to quieten Shirley. Helen bundled her through a change of clothing and we half-carried her to a waiting taxi.

All the way to the TV date she whimpered, but as we got to the Albany Club, where it was being broadcast, she started to shout:

'You've conned me into this!'

I abandoned all gentlemanly behaviour by pushing her, still yelling, into the ladies lavatory and going in with her.

Outside in the club, in front of the cameras Ron Randell, the show's compere, was filling in time waiting for Shirley to appear. Eddie Arnold, an impressionist on the show, heard the racket and he, too, came into the ladies. 'I know just how to deal with this,' he said after taking in the situation, and promptly gave Shirley a teeth-jarring crack on the jaw – her third slap of the evening. At this rate I was going to end up with a punch drunk singer.

By this time the place was filling up with people, all offering advice, all making things worse. Then through the crowd I heard a calm Lancashire voice demand: 'What are you doing with this girl?'

Jack Hylton pushed his way through, ordered everybody out of the room and put his arm around Shirley. As she cried on his shoulder he took a tranquiliser pill from his pocket and told her to swallow it. She did and Jack, talking quietly to her, walked into the club with her.

She took her place in front of the cameras and started to sing, her eyes still glistening from her tears.

I couldn't get near Shirley for the rest of the night. Jack Hylton made sure of that. 'Get away from her,' he said. 'You've done enough.'

As I quietly left the place I saw Shirley take her seat at Hylton's table. She looked at me and smiled... a superior, arrogant smile. The star was taking over the singer. Charitably I put it down to the tranquiliser and the champagne. I should have known better.

I must have felt sorry for the girl, because the following day I checked through her list of engagements and reluctantly called a few bookers with cancellations.

One engagement I left in was a 'double' at the Dorchester Hotel in London. It was near to home for Shirley and should not be too taxing. She was booked to appear in cabaret for a private dinner held by a boiler-making firm from Wolverhampton for its employees and their wives. There were so many of them that the dinner had been split into two separate parties, each a week apart.

On the first date Shirley was surprisingly nervous and when Tommy Trinder, one of the masters of off-the-cuff comedy who was the compere, came off stage he was baffled by the cool reception he had got. 'A lot of stuffed shirts,' was how Tommy dismissed the audience.

'Don't worry about it,' I reassured Shirley. 'Telling funny stories and singing are two different things. You'll paralyse them.'

She went on stage, wriggling along in her tightest dress. From behind the stage I listened to her first song and then the applause. It was good, but it dwindled after her second number and she finished the act to total silence.

Shirley was angry and mystified when she came off stage.

'Did you see that?' she asked me.

'See what?'

'The weird faces on those women. They looked so

disgusted. Was one of my boobs hanging out, or what? I don't understand it.'

'I do,' I said. 'At first the men were hanging over the backs of their chairs and they all had big, leery grins on their faces when they started applauding. Then the women got going on the men. They didn't like you. You were too sexy. That's why the men stopped clapping. They were frightened of those respectable wives.'

Two days later I was proved right. A letter from a director of the boiler-maker's firm said that there had been complaints from the women members of the entertainments committee about Shirley upsetting the wives and would she please not appear at the second party – but she would still get her fee for it.

We decided to accept the remarks as a compliment.

During those early months of 1956 Shirley was acting as if she was already swinging on her own personal star. She threw away her money on clothes she hardly wore and bought enough shoes for a centipede.

I had repeatedly told her that in the kind of career I had planned for her a long run in a West End theatre was just the first rung of a very long ladder, but she was behaving as if she were already at the top. The only thing to do was to jack her up a notch or two.

Immediately opposite my room at the Mapleton Hotel was the Cafe de Paris. Under the supervision of Major Donald Neville-Willing this plush London nightspot had developed a policy of presenting only the top world stars in cabaret – people on the level of Marlene Dietrich, Noel Coward and Eartha Kitt.

I wanted Shirley to appear there, to make an entrance down that beautiful curving staircase. The idea became an obsession and after one opening night at the cafe I cornered the Major.

'Just give the girl a break and I'll spend whatever you pay her on specially written material, costumes and publicity. Anything you say, I'll do,' I pleaded.

The white-haired, so precise elfin little man with a monocle smiled sweetly and said: 'I'll think about it, Mr Sullivan.'

I made sure that he did. Every time we met I gave his memory a prod. He was always polite, but never commital. As weeks passed I began to think I was wasting my time.

In the June of the year I was on holiday at Eze, near Monte Carlo, when I received a call from my secretary saying that the Major wanted to speak to me urgently about Shirley.

If there was a deal on the way I would be better off negotiating in London rather than at the end of a telephone, but I put in a call to him.

'Do you think,' he asked, 'that it would be possible for Shirley to open at the Cafe for the first two weeks of September?'

I gave my best imitation of a casual Riviera playboy: 'Well, I think we might prepare something in time.' With the hand that was not holding the telephone I was already beginning to pack.

That evening in London the Major and I settled the terms: two hundred pounds a week for two weeks, and the Cafe had the option to extend the engagement.

I was so delighted that Shirley had got the chance I had been praying for that I agreed with Neville-Willing when he added: 'You must understand that the Cafe de Paris is my baby. I shall tell Miss Bassey what to do and what to wear and which numbers are suitable for her to sing here.'

Inwardly I was determined that he should do no such thing.

The next problem was dealing with Jack Hylton. Under the terms of her Adelphi contract Jack had exclusive rights to Shirley's services and had to give his permission before she could appear at the Cafe.

Hylton and I had been drifting apart and in two months time he was to fire me when the first year of my contract came to an end.

I waited until Jack and I had parted and then asked him to allow Shirley to sing at the Cafe de Paris. I put a straight request to him – and got a straight answer:

'No.'

'Why?' I said.

'Because it will affect her performance in the theatre.'

'I don't think that's a very just argument, Jack. While she has been at the Adelphi you have used her many times on television and you've allowed her to play at other clubs.'

The answer was still 'No'.

I went back into battle with Jack two days later. By now he had softened a little and after a long argument he agreed to let Shirley sing at the Cafe ... on condition that he presented her.

'What do you mean "present"?' I asked.

'I have an act produced for her and on the programme it says "Jack Hylton presents"'.

Now I was caught between two people, Jack and the Major, both of them wanting to run the show.

'No,' I said. 'I don't think you know what's good for the girl. You have criticised me all along for my idea of building her as a sex symbol, so how can I believe that you'll produce the right act for her now?'

'I'm sure you would never spend the sort of money I intend to spend on her presentation. Nobody would. Anyway, no matter what you do I won't agree to it.'

We kept on talking and eventually Hylton said: 'How much is she getting?'

'Two hundred a week.'

'How long is the contract?'

'Two weeks.'

'All right. Pay me a hundred a week and I'll let her do it.'

I explained that there was an option to extend the engagement if the Cafe wanted to.

'Bugger the option. I'l be satisfied with the two hundred.'

I sent a cheque for two hundred pounds to Jack Hylton the following day and bought Shirley her first crack at real stardom ... for half of her wages.

I needed a really sophisticated song-writer to produce some original material for Shirley and got in touch with Ian Grant who had written for West End luminaries like Jack Buchanan, the Yacht Club Boys and for C.B. Cochran revues. I also engaged Les Paul, who had been the pianist for

Gracie Fields, to play for her, routine her songs and see her through rehearsals.

Ian, Les and I worked night and day to teach Shirley every trick we knew. I had a tight black gown with a band of mink around the bust made for her and went looking for the best orchestrator in the country. Everybody said Bill Oliver was the man and he agreed to arrange Shirley's music for the small Cafe de Paris band.

The Major was impressed by all this work and enthusiasm and decided to make Shirley's first performance an 'invitation only' night and insist upon evening dress.

The invitations went out to the aristocracy, the well-heeled, the socially acceptable and show business personalities.

During the rehearsals Shirley's opening was postponed because Liberace suddenly became available for the Cafe – but it gave us a chance to grab some more newspaper space for her.

While we were getting ready for the big night yet another problem came up. Shirley grew bashful when I told her she might be invited to join the nobility at one of the tables after the show.

'I can't. I just can't,' she moaned. 'All those knives and forks. I won't know what to do.'

It was time for me to put on another of the many hats an agent and manager has to wear: that of tutor in the social graces.

I took Shirley to one of London's best restaurants and for two hours I showed her how to sort the soup spoon from the fish fork and where the butter knife lay. I gave her hints about leaving the napkin in a jumbled heap and not folding it and warned her not to scrape the bottom of her cup when she stirred the coffee.

On Sunday, September 30 – the day before her opening night – Shirley was at the Cafe de Paris for her second dress rehearsal with the band.

It was a bad rehearsal and she did not get through it.

Ian Grant had written two new songs for her 'My Body's

More Important Than My Mind' and 'Sex'. There was also a parody version of 'Somebody Loves Me'. Everything depended on the WAY in which she sang the words. Without the right emphases and nuances the songs became meaningless.

Shirley, Les Paul and Ian had spent most of the rehearsal arguing about phrasing and then, when she was in the middle of an emotional ballad 'Who Are We?' the tears came.

The crying brought the rehearsal to an end, but I was not too worried about it. I considered it was probably the best thing that could have happened. Shirley had worked so hard preparing for her opening and had been getting more and more tense. The tears might bring a release at just the right time.

I put my arm around her and told her: 'Don't worry. I'll take you home and you can have a good rest.'

That night's sleep should have been the most vital in her professional life, but with an attitude and temperament as stormy as Shirley Bassey's events rarely follow a pre-ordained course.

The morning after that disastrous rehearsal I took a telephone call from 'Papa' Olivelli, the owner of the little hotel and restaurant where Shirley lived. 'Papa' was full of Italian excitement and told me Shirley was crying.

Within minutes I was at Olivelli's, in Store Street, just off Tottenham Court Road, and about half a mile from my Mapleton Hotel room.

At that moment all over London important people were ordering limousines, cleaning their tiaras and having their dress suits pressed, ready for an evening at the Cafe de Paris to see a glamorous young singer.

If they had got an eyeful of what I saw at Olivelli's they would have cancelled everything.

The glamorous young singer looked worn-out, puffy-eyed and as pale as anybody with her complexion could be.

I went over to her bedside and sailed into a gentle pep talk.

'Shirley,' I cooed, 'tonight you will have the world at your feet.'

She sniffed.

I began dropping names: 'Val Parnell will be there, and Liberace. Lords and ladies. You should be deliriously happy with this chance. Really, there's nothing to worry about.'

She blew her nose.

'It's nothing to do with the Cafe de Paris.'

'Then what...?'

The story came out. It was the jealous boy-friend again – the slap happy one.

When I had taken Shirley home the previous afternoon she had decided to relax by going to the cinema with Barry Hamilton, a young singer who also lived at Olivelli's.

'Afterwards we were having tea in my room,' she explained. 'Barry went to his room to get a book for me and while he was away there was a knock on the door and this other boy came in. I told him to go away and we argued. In the end I said, "I've finished with you, so will you please go."

'He said, "Well, you won't be seeing me any more", and I said "Good".

'He went out. I hear his car start up and roar down the road. Then there's silence. He must be turning. I hear it roaring back. Then a crash.'

Shirley often lapses to the present historic when she is excited. That and tears.

'I put my coat on and run downstairs. Two boys are in the doorway. One says "over there" and points across the road. There's that big petrol station over there and the car is rammed right into the gates.

'I was first there. I found him lying on the ground near the back of the car. I think he must have got out after the crash and collapsed. I lifted his head a bit and started crying. His face was covered in blood.

'The ambulance came and he got hold of my hand and kept saying, "will you go with me?" I said I would but Barry – he's there by then and he gets hold of our hands and unclasps them and says, "You can't. You've got the show to do tomorrow."

'Then people led me back to the hotel. I phoned the hospital this morning and he's on the danger list. I'll have to go to see him.'

There are times to be soft and times to be callous. This was one of the latter. I had to put a stop to this affair. I had never even seen this boy, but he had twice struck at my livelihood.

'You're not going near that hospital,' I said. 'Let it go. Finish it. There's too much at stake.'

Shirley for once took the point meekly. I think she was glad to have somebody else make that decision for her. Juhni, my wife, stayed with her until the final rehearsal at the Cafe at two in the afternoon and two hours later Shirley broke down again.

This time I did not let it bother me... at least it had nothing to do with fear of the big show that night.

I took her to the Adelphi and stood in the wings hoping that she would get through. One thing I was beginning to notice about this singer of mine was the way in which she could rise to the big occasion. She did two great shows at that theatre and when she was off stage I never left her alone for a moment. I cuddled her and praised her. All that hard work would not be wasted if I could help it.

We arrived in good time at the Cafe de Paris and the place was packed with the black and white of dinner suits and colourful evening gowns.

Shirley's eyes began to shine. When she reached her dressing room she was overjoyed at the sight of hundreds of telegrams from all kinds of celebrities. Flowers filled every corner and she looked as if she was in dreamland. I felt the same way myself. Even though I had sent all the telegrams and the flowers.

I watched while her dresser fitted her with earrings, necklace and a bracelet of diamonds, together worth ten thousand pounds and specially hired by me just for the opening night.

'I'm scared wearing all this fabulous jewellery,' said Shirley. No woman can roll her tongue around the words 'fabulous' and 'jewellery' the way Shirley can, especially when they run together in one phrase. She made a meal of it.

'Don't worry. There's a detective watching you all the time,' I lied. 'If you try to get away with it you won't get far.'

I left her and went to the balcony where Juhni was at a table with Hyman Zahl, the agent. I was too excited to sit, so I stood throughout the show.

That evening, with all of Shirley's problems, was made even more tiresome by the fact that downstairs at another table was Lily Berde, a beautiful Greek dancer.

In addition to Shirley I was now managing the far less troublesome affairs of Lil, singer Robert Earl and Armand, a one-armed lion-tamer who now did a budgerigar act.

But Lily had become more than a client and I had not yet broken the news to Juhni.

I wanted to share this night with my new love on the floor below, but at the same time I wanted to share it with Juhni who had done so much and put up with so many financial sacrifices to help launch Shirley.

The forefront of my mind was concerned with Shirley's act while another part of my consciousness was going through a schizophrenic tussle over Juhni and Lily. It was enough to spoil a perfect moment and I had only myself to blame.

I stayed on the balcony and watched Shirley walk down those famous stairs and start her first number. I whispered every word, every syllable, as she sang it.

She had them by the second number. After that she could no nothing wrong. She waggled her head and waved her hands with those long, tapering fingers and she scorched those white shirt fronts with her songs. Liberace's Mom held a lace handkerchief in front of her son's eyes and brother George put his fingers in Liberace's ears.

At the end I ran downstairs and stopped by the table that Lily was sharing with some friends. In her deep, heavily-accented voice Lily said: 'I am very happy for you. Now I am leaving.'

She went away and left me to share the great occasion with Juhni. Within forty-eight hours Juhni and I were to split for good.

Before going to Juhni I walked over to Shirley who was taking her last bow. As the applause washed over her I picked her up in my arms and carried her to her dressing room shouting 'We've done it Shirley!'

In the dressing room she started to cry again – but this time it had nothing to do with the boy in the intensive care ward.

Liberace came into the dressing room and asked Shirley: 'Is this all your own work?'

'Oh no, my manager Mr Sullivan here has put the act together and organised everything.'

'He's done a wonderful job,' said Liberace. 'You owe him a lot. Don't ever part.'

In the light of what was to happen later, I do not think she could have been listening.

I left Shirley to enjoy her triumph with her mother who had travelled from Cardiff for the opening night and went on to another night club, Churchill's in nearby Bond Street, to have a drink and talk out the night with Philip Ridgeway, the publicist who had handled the publicity for the opening.

Philip Ridgeway had also arranged the hire of the jewellery and he had told me to make sure that the baubles were put back in their boxes the second Shirley came off stage. During our conversation he suddenly asked:

'Did you bring the boxes?'

'What boxes?'

'The ones with the diamonds in.'

I did not stop to answer. I left Churchill's and bolted back to the Cafe de Paris. When I got there chairs were being piled on tables and people were sweeping up.

I ran into Shirley's dressing room and ransacked the place. I found the boxes but there was no sign of the jewellery. It looked as though we were going to start our stay at the Cafe even deeper in debt than I thought.

All I could hope was that Shirley still had the diamonds and I went home, determined to worry about it in the morning.

I was awake as soon as there was a decent amount of daylight, bought the morning papers as soon as I could and took them back to the Mapleton to read all the sensational things the critics were saying about my girl.

Then I called on Shirley, fingers crossed, to ask about the diamonds.

In her room at Olivelli's she told me: 'Everybody went and

there was just my mother and me and I said, "What about the diamonds? Where's Mike? Where's the detective?" I didn't know what to do so I took the stuff with me. I thought I would get as far as the door and the detective would come out of the wall.

'We got to the door. Nothing happens. We got up the street, into the hotel. I thought I wouldn't sleep with all this jewellery. In the end I locked the door and the windows and put the stuff under my pillow.

'Never, please, never hire any jewellery for me again.'

She lifted her pillow and there was all the lovely gleaming finery. I counted it twice, put it in the boxes and carried them back to Ridgeway.

Shirley's Cafe de Paris success extended the interest in her in two widely divergent directions. The glossy society weeklies, The Sketch and The Tatler, ran full-page studio photographs of her that made striking contrasts with the surrounding shots of county types whooping it up at hunt balls and the columnists of the mass-circulation daily and Sunday papers – always anxious to present themselves as world-weary, baggy-eyed habitues of the exclusive night spots – jumped firmly on her band wagon.

Major Donald Neville-Willing never changed the act and at the end of the two weeks he took up his option and Shirley stayed at the Cafe de Paris for nine weeks.

One day the Major called me into his office for a talk. He had been looking after Shirley as if she was his own daughter and she had responded by giving him the impression that I was robbing her.

I was just about to ask him to increase Shirley's money when he said: 'Do you think you are being quite fair?'

He was so convinced that I was making out of our deal that I had to put all the figures on paper for him.

My contract with Shirley allowed me to pay her nothing for working at the Cafe. In fact I was giving her an extra twenty five pounds a week. I was also paying Jack Hylton, the pianist, her dresser and the publicist. In addition there were four new songs – some at seventy five pounds, some at one hundred and fifty – the new gown, the jewellery hire and two visits to the hairdresser each week for Shirley. Entertaining newspapermen and bookers who came to the Cafe was costing me about thirty pounds a week.

But the end of the nine week engagement I stood to lose four hundred pounds.

Neville-Willing studied the pencilled figures.

'Shirley never told me you paid for all these things,' he said. 'She's a very lucky girl.'

But I never got the increase.

What I did get was a flood of offers for Shirley. Some of these came from abroad and I seized on them as the next rung of the ladder. From the start I had set out to ensure that Shirley's fame would be international. Many British offers promised more money. Some day money would be the objective. But not now. Now we simply wanted the world.

The first overseas job came in December when the show at the Adelphi ended. It was a broadcast from the Olympia Theatre in Paris and although the trip was one that was full of problems it was also one of sheer delight for both of us.

Scene Three: International Stardom

Shirley had never been out of Britain before and she was like a little girl, full of wonder and excitement. The Christmas spirit must have grabbed me because when we arrived at her hotel in Paris I told her: 'Shirley, you are getting one hundred pounds for this broadcast. For once I suggest you take the whole damn lot and go shopping.'

Her enjoyment was so infectious that I did not regret it and I even enjoyed standing for hours while she went through the usual feminine performance of seeing everything in a shop and then choosing the thing she first thought of.

Les Paul was scheduled to arrive with the music the next day, but London Airport was closed because of fog and there was no way – not even by train – that he could get to Paris in time for the show at seven that evening.

Without a pianist and without the music I explained the problem to our agent in Paris Eddie Marouni.

'Don't worry,' he said. 'The boys in the band will be able to fix you up.'

The Olympia's twenty-six musicians did a magnificent 'busking' job on 'I Can't Give You Anything But Love' and 'Stormy Weather' and got Shirley through the rehearsal with the rhythm and brass section having a kind of jam session while she sang a few notes to give them her right key.

By the time we returned for the evening broadcast someone had cobbled together a score for the fiddles. Shirley went like a bomb.

But our troubles in Paris were not over. Because of the fog we had decided to return to London by train and the only way we could make it so that Shirley could appear in Britain the next day was to dash from the Olympia to the station by taxi the moment the broadcast was over.

I had a cab waiting, but a gendarme moved it on and when I found another he managed to graze a truck about a hundred yards from the station. The damage was slight, but the argument was loud and long enough for us to miss the train.

When we did get away from Paris the next day we left with an offer of a month's engagement at the Olympia at three hundred and fifty pounds a week. The day was eventually fixed for the following May. It could have been sooner, but a new and exciting deal matured.

While Shirley had been at the Cafe de Paris an American called Sammy Lewis flew into London. Lewis was the entertainments manager of the New Frontier Hotel in Las Vegas. Years before he was part of an act called The Cycling Lewises and at one time had played the Cafe de Paris.

Nostalgia can press as hard on a trick cyclist as any one else and one night Sammy pedalled into the Cafe with Sol Shapiro, a director of the powerful William Morris Agency in America, riding tandem.

The New Frontier had a spot in its cabaret from January 23, and Lewis decided that Shirley could fill it nicely. He normally booked through the Morris agency and the following day he called on the agency London representative, Harry Foster of the Foster Agency.

Lewis and Shapiro went back to the States and Harry Foster sent for me to tell me he was going to America and would find other work for Shirley there. When he returned he had other offers for her, including one from Ciro's in Hollywood. I tied Shirley to the William Morris Agency for ninety days and it was, without my knowing it at the time, a good move. A week before we were due to fly out the New Frontier went into liquidation and the agency fixed Shirley into a more established venue – El Rancho. Sophie Tucker, Eartha Kitt and Joe E. Lewis were the sorts of stars who had appeared there.

Around this time Shirley fired the first shot in what was to become a long and tempestuous battle.

'Mickey,' she said. It was Mickey now, not Mister Sullivan.

'Yes?'

'I'd like a mink. And a car. A lovely, long, low Jaguar. A white one.'

'Oh,' I said, very non-commital... and wondering where I was going to get the fare money to America.

Minks and Jaguars were way out of my league as I tried to scrape that money together and in the end I had to borrow it from my accountant who advanced me the price of the fares plus two hundred pounds 'mad' money. That seemed enough because when we got to America Shirley would start earning enough to pay our expenses and our fares home.

But a last-minute complication arose – and this time it was my fault, not Shirley's. I was running away from my third wife Juhni and my second wife had chosen this moment to put on the pressure for a little back alimony that I had been unable to find.

Her solicitor was a real powerhouse when it came to working for a client, although it has always been my contention that the man could not see any further than his nose. It must have been obvious to him that my only chance of earning enough to pay the alimony was to go to America with Shirley. But he obtained a warrant to prevent me from leaving the country and it turned up at London Airport in the company of two very obvious plain clothes men.

I had arrived at the airport with Shirley, Jimmy Hyams, an old friend who was seeing us off, and Lily Berde – my new love who was coming with us.

From one end of the airport lounge I saw the two men. I guessed that they were police... and I guessed they were looking for me.

I sent the girls ahead to the departure lounge and asked Jimmy to check my baggage through. Then I took a deep breath and strolled over to the waiting pair.

'Are you in the job?'

'That's right,' one of them said.

'Me too. I'm from Streatham. I suppose you're looking for Sullivan?'

'Yes.'

'You know about the switch?'

'What switch? What's happened?'

'Well, I'm probably closer to it than you. I've been to his mother's house in Streatham, and he's going tomorrow on the morning flight. Number six four two.' I invented the number and hoped they would not check it. I thought also that they might unmask me by asking for some identification but an alimony debt case seemed such an insignificant matter and the wanted man was the last person they would expect to walk up and talk to them.

One of them said: 'We've been sent down for this flight.'

'So was I, but after what his mother told me I checked and he was taken off the passenger list an hour ago. I'll have to be here in the morning. Will you?'

'Suppose so. What time is the morning flight?'

'It's early, leaves at seven', I lied again.

They looked a bit lost, but patiently so, like many who are used to disappointments. I said: 'It's no good hanging around. Coming for a drink?'

In the bar I tried to keep the conversation to general subjects, but they began talking police shop. I kept my end up by mentioning one or two break-ins in Streatham and said I had been on a homosexual case and was glad when I was taken off because I hated that sort of work.

A couple of more drinks and I told them I was going home to my wife and arranged to meet them in the morning. They offered me a lift to South London but I made the excuse of having to telephone home which would take some time.

As they left I walked on wobbling legs into the departure lounge. A few minutes later I joined Shirley and Lily on the plane.

Our arrival at New York ran into a slight hitch when, at the immigration centre, Shirley was asked to wait while Lily and I went through in our turn. Shirley was kept waiting until everybody else had passed through.

For the first time Shirley had come up against America's sensitive colour question, but – fortunately – she did not realise the significance of it then.

Once I had asked her about discrimination and she told me: 'It means nothing whatsoever.

'Perhaps my mother being white made a big difference to me. When I was a kid other kids used to call after me "Blackie" and "Nigger, nigger come to dinner".

'Always the same things, but I soon put a stop to that because I could punch them. I didn't cry. I punched. Let them cry.

'When I was touring in those cheap shows landladies at digs would sometimes say they were full up, trying to be polite about it. I just turned my back and never let it get the better of me.

'Now if I go into a place and people stare at me I never think it's because I'm coloured. It's because I look attractive and striking when I'm wearing a wonderful gown. Otherwise it would drive me mad.

'Now I'm a star I'm never embarrassed.'

A star! The girl was really believing it. I should have seen the storm warnings, but I was too busy polishing that star.

We were five days in New York. Shirley had the time of her life.

My first visit in New York was to Columbia Records, who represented Philips (Shirley's London recording company) in America. With a lot of gentle persuasion and hard selling I arranged a recording session later in the week for her with Mitch Miller, then the world's greatest director of pop records. Shirley was given two lyrics to learn before the recording date.

For the first two days Shirley hardly left her hotel room. It had a TV set facing the bed, fitted with more channels than she could resist, and she began catching up on all the old films she had not seen.

I did nothing to discourage this. It was a free form of amusement and I had little enough money to throw around. But her addiction proved fatal to one of my deep-laid plans and almost wrecked another.

Through Lily, I had arranged to take a Mr and Mrs Zlotowski to dinner. Mr Zlotowski was in the jewellery business and I thought I might get some publicity out of a stunt similar to that which had worked at the Cafe de Paris by borrowing a fortune in diamonds for the Las Vegas opening at El Rancho. I had in mind something like a quarter of a million dollars worth and all I needed was for Shirley to charm these people with her girlish chatter over dinner to soften them up enough for me to introduce the idea of borrowing the jewellery.

Our date was for seven thirty. Shirley appeared at nine. She had been so interested in an old movie on TV that she wanted to see how it ended – and to hell with the Zlotowskis.

I went to her room to drag her to the bar, lost my temper and gave her a five-minute tongue lashing.

This left her in one of her most awkward and truculent moods. At New York's Brussels Restaurant she decided she was not hungry, answered questions in monosyllables and made it impossible for our guests to make easy conversation. It was like being with a spoiled child and when the time came at which I had intended asking for the loan of the jewellery, I sat dumb.

My relationship with Shirley was entering a very tricky period. Familiarity was beginning to breed contempt. When we met I was, admittedly, in a fairly small way as an agent. But she was in no way at all as a performer and to her I looked pretty big. I was Mister Sullivan. Now I was Mickey and the way things were going this was soon to be reduced to Mouse.

Shirley had no idea of the work I had put in, the long hours of bargaining, the stunts I had pulled to bring her along so fast. True, she had the voice and the stage personality to make it all worth doing, but I had been the one who had done it.

The idea was just entertaining Shirley's mind that she was a major star and that I worked for her – although it was to be some time before she actually put this thought into words. Her new fame was bringing her into continual contact with important and rich people and I did not dare let her know how my finances stood, that the gamble was still on and far from won.

So, in New York, while I ate cheaply and watched TV for amusement I provided the money for Shirley to be shown the town by a young publicity man named Ed Gollin. He took her to see one of her heroes, Sammy Davis Jnr in 'Mr Wonderful' and afterwards she was introduced to Sammy who surprised her by saying: 'You're the young lady who's been saying nice things about me.'

He was referring to a six-page feature about Shirley which had appeared in 'Ebony', the American Negro magazine and in which she had named him as one of her favourites.

Later Sammy Davis took her to dinner at a restaurant called Danny's Hideaway and to see Frank Sinatra's act at the Copacabana. Sitting at the same table as Sinatra after the show should have been a big thrill for Shirley. Instead she came back from the evening terrified.

The following day she told me how, with Ed Gollin, she was sitting at a table with Sinatra at its head:

'I leaned forward to look along the table and a woman flung me back and yelled "I wanna look at Frank". Every time I leaned forward somebody pushed me back.

'Sinatra had four tough looking men with him, to me they looked like gangsters, and he kept talking about Sinatra. The owner of the Copacabana, Joe Padella, sat next to me. He looked big and tough too.

'He gave me a dig in the side and said: "Wadda ya do?" I said "Sing". He said "Where?" I said "I open in Las Vegas next week". Then he said "Sing for me". I told him I couldn't because I had a contract and he didn't like that.

'He told me: "You can sing for Joe Padella" and he started getting mad and walking up and down. He said "Hey Frank, wadda ya think? She won't sing for me".

'Sinatra was busy talking about Sinatra and he just waved his hand and said "Never mind Joe, never mind". But I was getting scared and I whispered to Ed Gollin, "Let's get out here. These people frighten me".

I walked to the door with Ed, and Sammy Davis sent us home in his car. All the time I was expecting something awful to happen to me.'

At the end of our stay in New York we kept the recording date with Mitch Miller. It was a disaster.

Shirley had spent her time between late night outings and watching TV and had not properly learned the two lyrics she had been given. She had made excuses to get out of two rehearsal sessions with a pianist and when we got to the studio, on New York's East Side, Miller was, at first, concerned with the balance of the band. He changed the musicians' position and then started on Shirley.

Her lack of application was apparent. When she tried to record the songs her phrasing was wrong and Miller was furious.

'This is most upsetting. I'll be damn glad when the session's over. I have half a mind to cancel it,' he said.

It took so long to record the two songs that the band were on overtime rates and I had to plead with Miller not to drop everything.

'Please,' I said. 'She is a young girl. She has just arrived in New York for the first time. Try to see it our way.'

Shirley weighed in with some tears and he carried on. But at the end he said: 'I don't think it will be much of a record.'

By this time Shirley had stopped crying and hardened. 'Oh well,' she said haughtily, 'that's up to you isn't it.'

On the way to the hotel she turned to me and said: 'I thought they would have been a little more professional in America. In England Johnny Franz takes me over a number several times.'

'At one moment,' I told her, 'I thought Mitch Miller was going to take you over his knee.'

The one-armed bandits were there to greet us as we landed at Las Vegas – lined up like a guard of honour in the airport's entrance hall. It reminded me of a friend of mine, the American comedian Archie Robbins, who once said: 'The only way to beat Vegas is to get off the plane and walk boldly into the propeller.'

We drove by taxi to El Rancho, goggling at the huge, ever-open hotels with their neon signs. In our tinsel world this was close to the centre of the Universe. Here glamour reigned as it never would at the Hippodrome, Keighley. Enormous billboards announced the appearance of stars like Peggy Lee and Tony Martin.

Looking at names like that I was almost relieved when we arrived at El Rancho to see that Shirley's name was not in lights. As she stepped from the taxi she looked crumpled and tired... hardly the sort of thing to set the desert on fire.

Geri Nolan, the right-hand woman of El Rancho's owner Beldon Katleman, greeted us and arranged for our accomodation. Shirley was in a beautifully appointed wooden cabin in the grounds and Lily and I shared an adjacent one. The cost was fourteen dollars a day and the next morning Lily and I moved to an eight dollar a day motel. So far we had not earned one cent from the trip and the 'mad' money loaned by my accountant was disappearing fast.

Geri Nolan insisted that Shirley had a third gown with all the trimmings and I bought these at Las Vegas boom-town prices.

The opening night was different from anything Shirley had ever had to tackle before. She had to battle against the clatter of knives and forks as it was the Las Vegas custom to continue serving food during a performance.

I could not decide whether she had hit this audience of gamblers as hard as she had hit the people in Britain, but the critics reassured me.

Their reviews were ecstatic and I made sure that they were re-printed all over America by sending copies out to two thousand newspapers and magazines. Eight hundred of them reacted by mentioning Shirley's impact on Las Vegas.

All this cost money, but by now we were being paid by El Rancho and we at last had a little money left over to play with. Shirley's salary was one thousand eight hundred dollars a week. I gave her three hundred and fifty dollars of this, out of which she had her hotel bill to pay. I had to save as much as I could for fares to Hollywood after Las Vegas because the William Morris Agency had booked Shirley in Ciro's on Sunset Strip there.

With her pocket money Shirley quickly caught the

gambling bug. With Lily she fell hard for the one-armed bandits. I limited Lily's losses to just twenty five dollars a week, but I kept no check on what Shirley was losing and between 9.40 p.m. when her first show ended and one p.m. when her second began there was a gambling trap when there was nothing to do but play the tables and the machines.

Later I realised that I should have kept a closer eye on her, but right then I had another problem.

A few days after our arrival in Las Vegas Geri Nolan came to me and said: 'It is most important that you see Mr Katleman.' There was an undertone to her voice that disturbed me as I walked through the grounds of El Rancho to Beldon Katleman's apartment.

In his thickly carpeted suite Katleman lounged on a chair, wearing a white bathrobe, with his feet up on a cushioned stool. He invited me to sit down and then said:

'Mike, you don't know this town, do you?'

'I just got here, remember?'

Katleman, a hansome tanned Jew with a crew cut who looked every inch the big-time operator, did not smile. 'I understand you were seen around the town the other night with Miss Bassey.'

The night before I had shown Shirley and Lily the town and nodded. 'Do you mean she shouldn't have been seen in the other casinos before her opening?'

'No it's not that. It's just that if you are seen with her for more than a week in this town you are liable to be stoned.'

I sensed those words 'colour bar' but waited for him to say more – just in case I jumped to the wrong conclusion.

Katleman went on: 'It's not long since a white man dated a coloured singer here and he got beaten up.'

'You take note of this now. Tell your girl, too. You had better tell her because they're really hot on this in Vegas.'

First the wait at immigration and then this. If you move in the big money and big hotel circles you can travel a long way before it hits you, I thought, but now we had come up against it. I had no intention of making a martyr out of Shirley and it was easy to avoid taking her out myself because she was now working at night and I could plead business appointments during the day-time. I never told her about my meeting with Katleman.

Other men in Vegas knew the score and stayed away from her and it was this that particularly hurt Shirley. 'I can't understand it, Mickey,' she said. 'I've always had dates before. What's the matter with me?'

'It's your imagination,' I told her. 'And, anyway, not that many men have the time during the day and you work at night.' She seemed convinced and luckily she had her passionate affair with the one-armed bandits to keep her occupied.

During the middle of her run at El Rancho Shirley asked me to go with her one evening to the Dunes Hotel. She refused to tell me why and said she would not detain me for more than a few mintues.

I drove her to the hotel and we went along a corridor to the door of an apartment. As I knocked on it I still did not know what to expect.

We were greeted by two charming men who sat me down and offered me a drink. Then one said: 'We can assure you Mister Sullivan that it is well worth the money. We sell them to all the stars.'

'Sell what?' I asked, feeling that I was not going to like the answer.

'Minks,' said the man, smiling and spreading his arms. 'Hasn't Miss Bassey told you?'

Minks! In my financial state! I gulped down the drink and handed the glass back for a quick refill.

'Don't worry,' the man crooned. 'No sale has been made yet. We just showed Shirley a mink today and she liked it.' He opened a wardrobe and took out a dark brown mink stole. 'Including insurance, fifteen thousand dollars.'

Shirley grabbed the mink, threw it around her shoulders and began stalking the room with it, waving her hands and putting on her most haughty expression. 'All the chorus girls have them,' she said. 'I'll go without food...'

It hurt to tell her, but I had to: 'I'm sorry Shirl. We need all of our money for other things. I can't possibly buy it for you and I don't see how you can afford it.'

She took it so well. She handed the mink back and as we drove to El Rancho she told me: 'I suppose I was silly thinking I could buy a mink.'

I went back to my motel, thinking hard. When I got in I telephoned the salesman at the Dunes. 'I'll give you eleven thousand dollars for the mink,' I said. 'Three hundred down and a hundred a week.' Perversely, I now wanted Shirley to have it because she had behaved so well when I told her that she couldn't.

The salesman agreed and an hour later I walked into a Press reception that had been arranged for Shirley some days before and draped the mink around her.

From inside the fur a muffled voice asked: 'How *did* you get it, Mickey?'

'How did *you* get it, you mean. Get this straight. It's going to cost you a hundred dollars a week.'

She loved the idea and I thought it would cut down on her gambling because there wasn't much time left in her life after she had made a dozen trips every evening to her wardrobe to take out her new toy and stroke it, saying: 'This will go *fabulously* with my white Jaguar.'

The rest of our stay in Las Vegas went well and Beldon Katleman booked Shirley for the next two years at three thousand dollars a week for the first engagement and five thousand a week for her stint in the second year. People of the standing of Eartha Kitt and Sophie Tucker got eight thousand and this sort of money meant that my carefully planned career for Shirley was following the right lines.

Shirley never returned to Las Vegas under that deal because before we could take up our option the following year El Rancho was burned to the ground.

'A swimming pool,' Shirley specified as we drove to Hollywood for the dates at Ciro's. 'I want to stay in a place with a swimming pool.'

At the first five hotels we tried in Hollywood the prices were too high – swimming pool or not. The sixth was a plush apartment house with one apartment available and a pool. I went in alone to book it for her and then told the man on the desk: 'The apartment is not for me. It's for Miss Bassey. She is opening at Ciro's next week. Miss Bassey is coloured.'

The man never said a word. He just looked sorry. I got the message. I got out. At the car I told Shirley: 'Full up.'

Soon, however, I found her a pleasant apartment with a bar and a swimming pool in the ground for ten dollars a day. Lily and I found cheaper places.

Shirley's engagement at Ciro's was for six weeks at two thousand dollars a week and she was due to open three days later, on Saturday evening.

On our first evening in Hollywood I took Shirley to dinner at Ciro's so that she could see the place, the type of customers she would play to and the reception they gave to an artist.

She was excited by the huge illuminated 'C' outside, by the two doormen and the boy who came out to park our car, but her face fell when we got inside. It was a dreary room with cheap decor and business was terrible. I began to wonder how the unknown Miss Bassey would fare there when the brilliant American comedienne Frances Faye was playing to about thirty people.

Herman Hover, the owner, a typical night club boss with eyes all over the place, came over and introduced himself and I noticed with some relief that at least the house band was good.

But I need not have worried. Shirley with her big occasion temperament was at her most electrifying at the opening. She put the audience into a state of shock and they stopped eating and drinking, which is something in an American club. The newspapers labelled her 'the girl who livened up the Strip' and Ciro's did better business that it had before she arrived.

I counted the trip a success, but my joy was marred on our fourth day at Ciro's when Geri Nolan telephoned me from Las Vegas:

'Mike, what about this bill of Shirley's?'

I knew that Shirley had been paying her apartment bill week by week.

'It's all paid,' I said.

'Not quite. I have an outstanding account here of over six hundred dollars and Beldon's furious.'

Shirley, I learned, had been drawing heaps of dimes to feed the one armed bandits and this had been put on a separate bill which she had left unpaid.

'Geri,' I said, 'send the bill to the Morris office and I'll see that it's paid. It's just an oversight.'

'It's a six hundred dollar oversight and Beldon takes a dim view of it.'

Later I exploded with Shirley over the bill and then I had another battle with the Morris agency to get them to advance the money.

That six hundred dollar bill was the least of my money problems – although at the time I was not aware of it. Not until I went to Herman Hover for Shirley's two thousand dollar salary for the first week at Ciro's.

He handed me three hundred dollars, saying: 'Would you mind accepting this as cash. I'll give you the balance on Monday.' Hover had to pay the Morris agency commission of two hundred dollars, so I had fifteen hundred to come.

I gave two hundred and fifty dollars to Shirley and then started to worry about the weekly payment on the mink stole and my hotel bill. I had been there for eight days and the fifty dollars and a few cents in my pocket would not cover what I owed. When I moved in the management had asked for a week's rent in advance. I had talked my way out of paying it by telling them of the two thousand dollars to come from Ciro's. When I went back that afternoon and explained that I had not been paid yet the manageress accepted the situation – but under protest.

For the next three days I tried to get money out of Herman Hover, but I was continually put off with excuses and one night I got back to my room and could not push the key into the lock. It had been plugged with a block of metal. Indignantly I went downstairs and found a porter.

'I'm very sorry sir,' he said, 'but you haven't paid your bill. There's nothing I can do.'

'Where are my bags?'

The man looked embarrassed. 'Your luggage is all packed away.'

'A toothbrush?' I pleaded. 'A razor?'

The porter looked down and shuffled his feet.

I slunk out of the place and counted my cash. I had just five dollars and twenty cents... and a rising star earning two thousand a week!

That night was spent on the back seat of my hired car and in the morning I eased my creaking joints into the driver's seat and drove, unshaven, to Lily's hotel.

Lily, too, was on a tight budget but she managed to lend me enough to pay my hotel bill and to talk the management at her place, who had known her for years, into taking a chance on me.

I kept hounding Hover for money and it came in dribs and drabs... enough to pay Shirley, keep up the instalments on the mink and repay that six hundred dollars to the Morris agency.

I lived some days on nothing but coffee and doughnuts and kept my troubles from Shirley. She filled her time by taking driving lessons which took her all around the sight-seeing spots of Hollywood – and then she failed her test by driving through a red light. She soon righted that by getting a provisional licence which enabled her to keep driving around. The thirty dollars it cost would have made good eating money for me.

One night I was unable to get to Ciro's and the next morning Shirley told me: 'There were some men in last night, Mickey. They want to buy my contract. I said you would be in tonight and they said they would come back.'

'Are you interested?'

'Yes. They said they can get me into Las Vegas at much bigger money, but I don't mind if you do a deal with them where you stay in too.'

Already she was trying her arm, showing me that she was the important half of the partnership and that I, in her eyes, was just the labourer.

That night in Ciro's the head waiter told me: 'There are four gentlemen waiting for you over there.'

The description in no way fitted to two largest of the quartet and the third was too loudly dressed to qualify. The fourth, who turned out to be the leading man, was attractive and tanned. He wore a grey silk suit and showed a lot of white cuff. His short collar was high on the neck, fastened with a gold pin. His smile was a commercial for his dentist.

I walked over, sat down, refused dinner and accepted a drink. Grey silk slid over a few pleasantries, then laid it out.

'You know,' he said. 'We want to take over this girl of yours?'

'Shirley did mention it.'

'We are prepared to buy her contract for a lot of money. We own a piece of Vegas and we run a saloon there. We have a way, if we want somebody in, they're in. If we want them out, they're out.'

'Interesting,' I said. 'Do you represent an agency?'

They all laughed and then one of the supporting acts said: 'Listen son, if he says something's in, it's in.' Grey silk tried to look modest at this praise. 'We don't bother with agents. We have our own ways.'

'We have our own pressure methods, too.'

It was clear that these four were hoodlums and trying to make me believe they were very big-time hoodlums at that.

'I'll tell you what I'll do, gentlemen,' I said. 'I keep fifty per cent of my deal with Shirley and you give me seventy five thousand dollars for the rest. Go and see the lawyers at the Morris agency tomorrow and if you're serious buyers they'll no doubt show you the contract. That's the deal – and all negotiations through the Morris lawyers.'

I got up and left them. I never saw them again. You never do see that kind again, once you mention lawyers.

We left Ciro's, still owed money by Herman Hover and drove to Reno where the Morris office had booked Shirley into The Riverside Room at one thousand five hundred dollars a week. That money owing from Ciro's did not worry me too much. In my profession a sum owing from Hollywood amounted practically to a status symbol.

Shirley was happy in Reno. She was full of confidence now and able to do her act in the evening and then forget about it for another twenty four hours. Once she really worried me by staying out all night but she grabbed me the next day and happily bubbled out her story.

She had gone off to get married!

'You really mean that?' I shrieked. 'You didn't, did you? Tell me you didn't.'

'I didn't, Mickey, but I nearly did and I would have done. After the show I met this really good looking man and we had some drinks and the subject of marriage came up.

'He proposed and I got terribly romantic about it. I thought it was marvellous, being proposed to and I also thought that, being in Reno, I could get a quickie divorce before I leave, so I accepted.

'We went in his car and drove all over the place, talking about the wedding, for hours. He even got a friend of his with a radio station to congratulate us over the air, but there was no mention of a wedding.

'Then it got light and I thought: "Bit weird. He's got no intention of marrying me". All he wanted to do was take me home and get me into bed. What he did do was waste the whole night talking. Why couldn't he have just come out with it instead?'

Shirley got two more marriage proposals in Reno during her stay there . . . both at the same time and both from midgets.

It happened because one evening she saw a line of tiny men walking into the hotel as she went to her dressing room to prepare for the show. They were in Reno for a midgets' convention and while she was dressing a startling thought hit her:

'One of her songs was a parody on the old Cole Porter number 'Let's Do It' and contained the line 'even little men who have to reach do it.' She worried over the hurt this could cause and was struggling to think of an alternative line when the leader of a group of Morrocan acrobats who were on the same bill came up to her.

This man, Ben, was the one of the eight Moroccans who spoke English.

'Oh, Ben,' she wailed. 'I've just had the most dreadful revelation.' Shirley will never use one little word where two big ones will do.

She explained about the midgets and the line in the song. 'What can I do?'

Ben gave her an invaluable piece of advice: 'If you ever come face to face with somebody in the audience who might be affected by your lines don't try to change anything at the last minute. Just look them dead in the eye and smile. Say it... but smile.'

Shirley was doubtful, but when she came to the line she sang it loud and clear – and she looked at the midgets and smiled. They roared their approval and from that night on wherever she went in the hotel the two leading midgets trotted with her, one on each side, and both proposing marriage.

We had a week to go before we were due to take the plane home to England and I still did not have the fare money. Then good news came in letter from London from Johnny Franz, Shirley's recording manager.

Before we left London Johnny had talked Shirley into making a record of the calypso number 'The Banana Boat Song'. She did not want to do it, saying 'I don't want to be known as a calypso singer,' but Johnny told her there was no better material around at the time and persuaded her to record it.

The letter from Johnny told me that the song had gone into the Hit Parade and this meant that we should eventually earn some thousands of pounds in royalties.

I was thinking of calling Johnny and asking for an advance so we could cover the fares home, but I had a better idea. The news of Shirley's American success had been fairly widely circulated in Britain and the fact that she now had a record in the charts would raise her value at home.

I put in a call to Leslie Grade, the big variety booker and asked him: 'Would you like to present Shirley in variety?'

'Yes. I certainly would.'

'I want five hundred pounds a week and fifty per cent of the profits...'

'Sure, sure,' said Leslie.

'... and two air fares from Reno to London.'

'Done.'

Sullivan triumphs again!

Then I called Johnny Franz and asked him to meet Shirley at the airport when a big model boat with cellophane sails and a huge bow on top of the mast with Shirley's initials on it. And full of bananas. That, I thought, should make pictures for the papers and let people know Bassey was back.

When we touched down Johnny was there with the boat and the photographers.

We would have done better with a smaller boat. When the pictures dropped on editors' desks none of them could find room for all that shipping.

'Next time,' I told Johnny. 'More Bassey, fewer bananas.'

Shirley went from the airport to the May Fair hotel where she took a sixty pounds a week suite. The idea was to have plush surroundings where she could be interviewed and seen by agents and bookers.

She started thinking about what she could buy with that sixty pounds if she moved from the May Fair and she accepted an offer from the mother of the boy who had almost ruined her Cafe de Paris opening with his car crash to stay at her home and share a room with her daughter.

I was opposed to the move, considering what had gone before, but she assured me that she could handle the situation and I gave in.

What Shirley really wanted to do was to go home to Cardiff, see her family and hand out coming-home presents, but I had plans for Cardiff, where she was due to appear on the third week of her variety tour for Leslie Grade.

I was determined to turn her home-coming into a massive publicity stunt. I got a scoutmaster to organise his boys to meet her at the local railway station, along with one hundred and forty members of a youth club Shirley had belonged to for a short time. The scouts offered their band, so did the Girl Guides and the Boys' Brigade.

I accepted every offer on the grounds that three bands meant three big drums and this was definitely a three-big-drum affair.

British Railways agreed to label their engine 'Welcome Home Shirley Bassey' and I hired a magnificent open car for Shirley to ride in from the station.

Then the police stepped in.

It was Friday evening when I had a telephone call from a high-ranking cop saying: 'I understand that you have organised a parade along the High Street for Sunday.'

'That's right.'

'I'm sorry, but it can't be done. This is largely a community of churchgoers and you have arranged this for eleven o'clock in the morning – and without informing us.'

I said: 'May I come round and talk this over.'

'If you like,' said the man, sounding as though it made no damn difference to him where I went.

On the way to the police station I worked myself into an arrogant mood. Once there I told the man: 'This is the first time Cardiff has produced an international star. All these youngsters are ready to greet her and now you say I have to cancel it.

'Even if I wanted to do that I don't have the time. And I'm going ahead with it.'

'If you attempt to hold a parade on Sunday, Mr Sullivan, I shall have you put under arrest.'

'Do that,' I told him, 'and I'll get all the publicity I need. I am not going to do a thing to stop this welcome and if you do arrest me I hope you arrest Miss Bassey, too.

'I'll be back in Cardiff with her at eleven on Sunday morning.'

I returned to London early on Saturday as I took Shirley by train to Cardiff I told her nothing about the planned welcome or the policeman's threats.

When we got off the train the platform was packed five deep with the youth club members, the Boy Scouts, Girl

Guides, Boys' Brigade and their bands... and about six hundred other people lined the route to the Queen's Hotel half a mile away.

Shirley cried, accepted two bouquets that I had paid for and sat on the back seat of the limousine waving the way she had seen American Presidents do.

Her opening night at the New Theatre the following evening was played to a packed house.

Shirley closed the show with a speech, scripted by me, in which she thanked 'all the wonderful Welsh people' and then called her mother on to the stage to thank her for making everything possible.

I watched from the box, half hoping that she might mention the man who had made a lot of it possible – me.

But she did not.

What she did say, afterwards, was: 'Why do I have to keep working all the time? Can't I have a holiday? Tommy Steele has a car. Why can't I have a car?'

My best answer was that she had just failed another driving test.

It was at this time that Shirley started to make arrangements for her sister to adopt her little daughter Sharon. For three years she had been unable to make up her mind about the child. Before the baby was born she thought only of passing her on to her sister, who was childless after years of marriage.

When the baby came she began to think differently. For a while she went with the child to live with another married sister in North London and having to look after the baby's needs brought that age-old yearning to stay a mother. She did not want to let go.

Eventually the childless sister in Cardiff looked after Sharon and every time they met she asked Shirley: 'When are you going to sign the papers?'

Shirley, playing with the baby, would reply: 'Plenty of time.'

Sharon began walking and talking and every time Shirley went to Cardiff and saw her all of her resolution to sign the adoption papers would fade away.

In her mother's house there was a picture of Shirley and whenever it was shown to Sharon and she was asked 'who's that?' she would say 'Mummy'.

But when the little girl saw Shirley in person she did not link her with the photograph and called her 'Aunty Shirley'.

One day in Cardiff Shirley was playing with the baby when her sister walked in. Sharon turned her back on Shirley and ran to the sister, crying 'Mummy'.

Shirley realised the time had come to sign those papers...

Shirley's sex life was something I had tried to keep out of ever since the beginning of our professional relationship.

In retrospect it would have been better if I had kept a closer eye on her. Whenever she was in London she continued to live at the home of her ex-boy friend, 'Pepe' Davis. Other men called there for her and took her out and if I had not been so busy with her professional affairs I would have smelt the trouble that was brewing.

My relationship with my new star was becoming a little strained because she had cottoned to the fact that she was a somebody. Although her contract called for her to get sixty five pounds a week she demanded more money and – after talking to my accountant – I increased it to one hundred and twenty five.

I also arranged for her to buy a house for her mother in Cardiff. It cost four thousand pounds and Shirley planned to pay for it quickly, in large monthly sums. This was done by me making deductions from her earnings and the method led to even more squabbles between us.

After her provincial variety tour ended I had arranged performances for her in Stockholm, Belgium and Monte Carlo. My scheme for 'internationalising' Shirley was moving along well.

The engagement at the Sea Club in Monte Carlo was for seven days and immediately on arriving on the Riviera Shirley found herself a young Greek named Nicky, the son of a millionaire ship owner, and spent her days touring in his car or sailing on his yacht.

Before appearing at the Sea Club, Shirley had one

performance to do – a very lush affair at Monte Carlo's Sporting Club, which put on a gala evening every Friday during July and August.

Even millionaires give a tug to their black bow ties and straighten their shoulders as they walk into that pillared pleasure palace and it is renowned for the fact that the world's greatest entertainers are ignored by the clientele who are usually more interested in who is wearing whose wedding ring before they finish their meals and get down to gambling on the only tables in 'Monte' without any limits.

Shirley came out to sing... and flopped.

But she never knew it because I had told her that the acoustics of the place were such that any applause floated out to sea and the performer could hardly hear it.

At the Sea Club she was a riot and her young Greek came into watch her every night and take her out every day.

An old friend of mine, Bob Squachiaficci, was the Mayor of nearby Eze and the proprietor of a hotel there. He had invited Shirley and I to dinner. Shirley was out with her boy friend on the day we were due there and did not return until an hour after we should have started out.

I was angry with her and showed it. She got ready quickly enough, but I was in no mood for forgiveness as we set off in my open sports car.

On the way I kept grumbling: 'What the hell do you think you're doing? These people are preparing a lovely meal for you... a privilege for us both... the height of rudeness to be so late... if you'd rather go out with some boy...'

'Of course I'd rather go out with a boy,' she yelled. 'Rather than have dinner with somebody I don't know, who's already married anyway. Don't you think I might want to get married to somebody some day?'

We were now about six miles out of Monte Carlo when she said: 'Anyway, I don't want to meet your friends.'

'You can be sure,' I bellowed, 'that they don't want to meet you.'

I pulled over to the side of the road, leaned across her and opened the door.

'Out.'

She got out. From the dark, deserted roadside, huddled in her mink, she said: 'What's this?'

'I'm not taking you any further.'

'How do I get back?'

'Walk.'

'I don't know the way. At least give me some money for a taxi.'

'There are no taxis where you're standing.'

I slammed the door and drove off to a late dinner.

For Shirley our row was the beginning of a comedy of errors that amused her so much that she actually forgot to be angry with me when she came running the next day to tell me about it.

'There was me,' she said, 'standing by the side of the road in the dark. I thought "all I can do is walk" and I walked. For hours. I came to the town and then to the dock where all those big yachts are. As I went across the road this big American car passes and I recognise the boy at the wheel. It is Nicky. There was an older man beside him, probably his father. I waved and he ignored me. Went on past.

'The car stopped by the yachts and they get out. I'm leaning by the wall. I think maybe he ignored me because he was with his father. Then he came back and went to talk to some people at a bistro. I'm smiling at Nicky and nothing happens. I am furious.

'I go to the club, and do my act and afterwards I get changed and go into the bar. Nicky is there.'

In the bar Shirley went into her hurt and outraged act until a bewildered Nicky explained that the man she saw must have been his twin brother who had never seen her, or heard about her.

'We both laughed,' she said, 'and I had a double brandy right away.'

Shirley and the young Greek had fallen very heavily for each other. I later learned that when the time came for her to return to London they had a very romantic parting when Nicky left on his father's yacht – 'Goodbye... don't turn around.' That sort of performance.

When she opened later at the London Hippodrome there was a bouquet of red roses from him with a card saying 'Pound of sugar', a phrase Shirley used as a child as the answer to 'How much do you love me?'

But they never met again.

The Hippodrome show was a two week run at the top of a variety bill. I set out to make Shirley's return to the West End larger than life and paid David Jacobs, then Britain's top disc jockey and pop music TV personality, seventy five pounds a week to introduce her.

Leslie Grade, who was backing the show, was horrified at some of my more outlandish ideas, like having Shirley emerge from a giant cut out picture of herself, but agreed to go along with it.

Then Shirley herself stepped in and almost ruined the whole extravaganza.

On the Monday shortly before she was due to open at the Hippodrome she came to me and said: 'I'm having a new gown for tonight.'

I had selected a gold lamé dress, very tight, with a halter neckline and a split down the front almost to the waist.

'I know you are,' I said.

'No. I don't mean the one you've chosen. I've ordered one myself.'

A little surprised, I asked to see this creation and was told it was at her dressmakers' whose attic workshops were just yards from the theatre's stage door. Shirley said she was going there and I agreed to follow within a few minutes.

When I walked up the winding stairs to the workroom and opened the door I saw Shirley standing in a white crinoline with a diamante top. The skirt filled the small room. I didn't believe it. I went outside, closed the door and counted to ten. I went back in and told her:

'You've got to be the first black Cinderella I've seen in all my years in this business. Get it off.'

Shirley began to shout. I shouted louder.

'You are not wearing that tonight, so forget it.' I returned

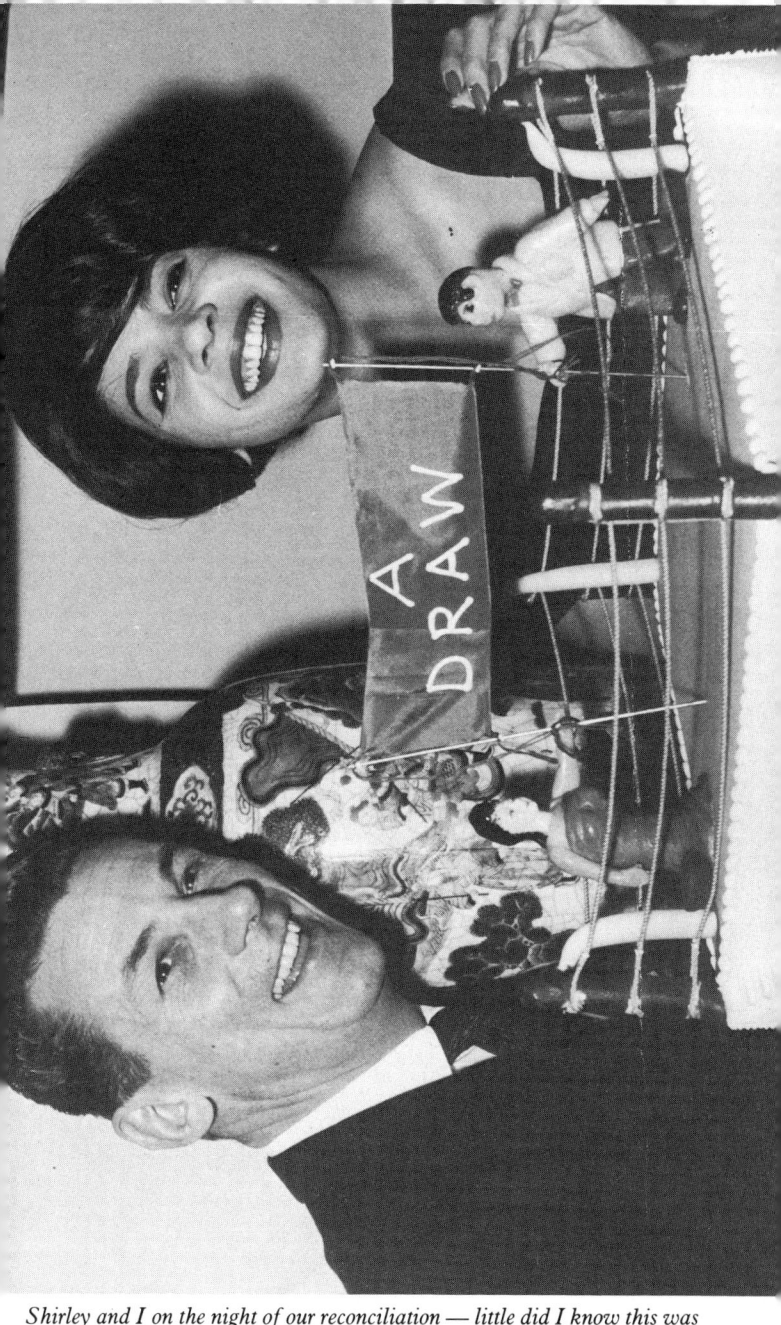

Shirley and I on the night of our reconciliation — little did I know this was only the end of round one!

Shirley Bassey with her first husband, Kenneth Hume, after their wedding.

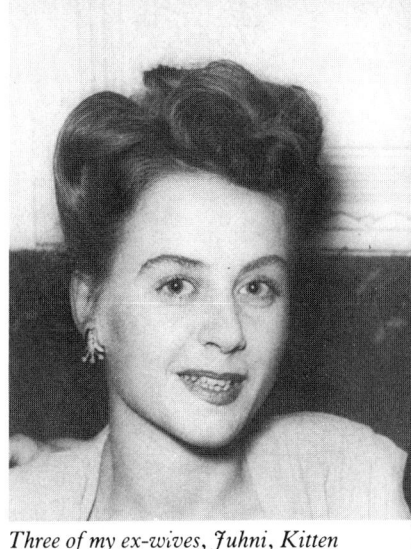

Three of my ex-wives, Juhni, Kitten and Lily and now three of my best friends.

Dany Robin and "Hitch" getting on like a house on fire just after our house had burnt to the ground and with George Saunders in "The Best House in London", both stars broke up when George put his leg down the wrong side of his trousers

A happy day, with happy clients, at my wedding, to Dany, 23 November,

Ted Rogers, I kept my promise and he became a star. Des O'Connor — blame him too if you are not enjoying the book so far! Having a ball on our wedding day.

Dany with her grandchildren Dian and Ayde at our home in Marbella. The two of us in front of a model of the Bounty ship.

Wedding number five — now and forever.

to the theatre and gave orders that no white crinoline dress should be allowed in on any account.

Shirley went on that night and every night in the gold lamé.

Scene Four: Press Revelations

The Hippodrome audiences loved the extravagant presentation of Shirley. It was ostentatious... but then Bassey IS ostentatious. At the end of every performance I has sixteen bouquets brought on stage for her – all paid for by me. The Hippodrome had more flowers than acts that fortnight.

As the show neared its end I managed to catch pleural pneumonia, but talked my doctor out of sending me into hospital and carried on working from my bed at the Mapleton Hotel.

Being sick was not helped by the fact that Shirley had started behaving in a very demanding manner. That 'star' label was really getting to her.

She was twenty years old, she was reading the posters I had written which said she was a fabulous star and she was living the part in the way she saw it.

Getting her to rehearse a new song was like leading a reluctant schoolgirl to her lessons. She was temperamental with theatre musical directors and one day she cost Philips Records a lot of money by going to her hairdresser instead of keeping a recording date and leaving forty musicians cooling their heels in the studio.

On another occasion she walked out of a BBC-TV 'Six Five Special' show because she was told she could not keep her dog, a white miniature poodle called Beaujolais, in her dressing room. She went back later, but not until the producer, the director and the band had passed a panic-filled three hours.

At one early morning incident in a night club, the 21 Room, Bertie Meadows, the owner, was the loser. There was an argument over a bill.

As Shirley described it: 'I went to the club with my friend Verne O'Hara and Mr Keith Hamilton. Nobody was high. I only drank red wine. My girl friend was drinking ginger beer and Mr Hamilton had three gin and tonics. The bill came to eight guineas, including three pounds ten shillings for eggs and bacon. I come from a family who live on eight pounds a week.

'I had a little argument with Mr Meadows. He yelled all over the room like a baby whose mother has taken his toys away.'

And the slap?

'His head just happened to be where my hand went. It wouldn't have hurt a baby.'

Over to Mr Meadows, hurt, upset and relaxing in a Turkish bath: 'Miss Bassey was drinking port and the others whisky. Two of them ate eggs and bacon and the other half a chicken. Miss Bassey tore up the bill and said something about a clip joint. I can still feel where she hit me.'

I sent Meadows a cheque to cover the bill.

Privately, with me, Shirley was also playing the star and the strain of dealing with her and her temperament added to the life-style I led, caught up with me.

While she was away on a variety tour, an X-ray revealed that I had tuberculosis. But the specialist could not keep my mouth from moving and I had two extra telephones installed at the bed-side so that I could carry on working.

Almost immediaely I got an offer of an engagement in Australia for Shirley and although she was booked for months ahead I decided to cancel other dates and try to conquer another continent.

The Australian trip meant that my time in bed would be six weeks and not six months.

During that time my rarest visitor was Miss Bassey. She came around to eat my grapes only three times and when I telephoned her she was curt and cold.

I realised that she was slipping out of my grasp and anyone who had anything to murmur into her ear took the opportunity while I was not around to interfere.

Sometimes these were simple murmurs, such as: 'I don't think you should appear at Brighton – it's not your kind of town'. Then, within twenty-four hours Shirley would be telling me: 'I don't think I should play Brighton.'

I could talk her out of matters like that, but there were the more serious murmurers, the people who saw a gold-mine in the girl now that I had half killed myself clearing away the layers of top shale and reached the pay dirt.

One of these was an American who claimed to be the manager of a big singing star. He was dating Shirley and sent her a case of champagne and bought her a gown for seventy pounds.

By contrast, I was the man who was stopping huge chunks of her income to pay for the house she was buying. One day, in a temper, she screamed at me: 'What good is a manager who's lying on his back all day?'

I had to get out of that bed and back into the driving seat.

Shirley's love life also lead to her changing addresses. The woman in whose house she was living telephoned me to say she had told Shirley to leave because her son could no longer put up with seeing her go out on dates with other men and she considered Shirley a bad influence on the boy.

While Shirley moved into an hotel I was arranging to go to Australia to set up advance publicity for her. My TB specialist was not happy about this and I compromised by agreeing to fly across the world in easy stages, with long rests in between.

I knew that if I did not go I was going to lose Shirley Bassey. Her attitude towards me had hardened into one of mistress and servant and her arrogant and high-handed attitude had turned a number of people against her.

Two days before I left for Australia I left my bed and went shakily to a band call for Shirley at the Bagatelle Club in Mayfair where I had booked her.

Shirley was more difficult than usual that morning. She simply blew her top, declared that the music was all wrong and that she had outgrown Les Paul, one of Britain's top accompanists, who was playing for her.

For the first time I did not have the energy to shout her down. She stormed out and I was unable to stop her. As I leant against the piano, sick and shaking, trying to placate Les, people gathered around and told me: 'Don't worry, she'll turn up.'

She did arrive for the opening and her stay at the Bagatelle was a successful one, but on that first night I felt there was no life or sparkle in her songs.

I arrived in Australia ten days before Shirley and spent my time appearing on TV shows and countless radio programmes talking about her and making friends with newspapermen.

Everything was set for a well-publicised arrival when, at three a.m. on the morning before Shirley was due to fly out from London, I got a telephone call in my hotel room that was to lead to Shirley getting more publicity than I had dreamed of.

Clyde Packer, the son of Australian newspaper owner Sir Ralph Packer, was on the line from the office of the Sydney Daily Telegraph.

'Mike, you had better get around here. We've just had a flash on an agency tape. It says "Shirley Bassey in shooting".'

I struggled awake. 'What else does it say?'

'Nothing else yet. It's just the first flash and it gives us a chance to re-scheme a page if we want to. It may be a while before we get the full story.'

I rushed to the Daily Telegraph office in Castlereagh Street, but when I got there there was still no more news. I tried to telephone London but could not get through and after a galling wait the first version of the story came over – a sketchy account of Shirley being locked in a hotel room with a gunman. At the end it was still not clear whether she was alive or dead.

Two hours after that first flash a full version of the story dropped. Shirley was unhurt and later in the day there were wired pictures of her leaving London Airport for Sydney.

At Sydney Airport the next day there were three TV crews and about thirty newspapermen waiting on Shirley. She stepped out of the plane and stalked coldly past the banners, flowers, cakes and kangaroos I had laid on to sneer at me: 'Fancy sending me tourist class on a thirty-six hour flight.'

When reporters asked her about the shooting she became even more abrasive. 'Don't want to talk about it,' she snapped. 'Had enough shooting. You ever been in a shooting? You ought to try.'

I tried to sooth the ruffled Press men but nothing I could do would make her amenable. We had parted on bad terms over the incident at the Bagatelle Club, and then the shooting...

But I introduced her to a man called Bruce Gordon, the general manager of the Tivoli theatres in Australia. He was tall, he was handsome and he soon impressed Shirley. I let him take over and under his guidance she became more pleasant and started to talk to the reporters.

Later on Bruce's influence on Shirley became even more marked. Their relationship developed into a warm love affair and for a time there was even talk of marriage.

After Shirley had rested and settled down and we had renewed an uneasy friendship she told me about the shooting:

'I went out with a boy called Peter Quinton on and off during the last week I was in London,' she said. 'On Sunday night, the night before I was due to fly out, Peter and I went to the cinema.

'He came back to the hotel to help me pack. The boys (I knew she meant her two dressmakers) were coming over to bring my new gown.

'We were packing when the phone rings and there's this phoney American accent.

' "You Shirley Bassey?" and I answered "Yes".

' "I've got a bouquet of flowers here for you and I'd like to deliver them".

'I said "How come you're delivering flowers at midnight?"

'He said: "Well, they were left here and we can't hold them any longer. Would you mind telling me your room number?"

' "If you've got flowers take them home to your mother".

'He said "My mother's in Texas, Ma'am".

' "Your mother's in Bayswater. I know who you are." '

She had recognised the voice of the boy at whose home she had been living before his mother had kicked her out.

'I went into the bathroom to take off my make-up and told Peter to ask who it was if anybody knocked on the door. There was a knock, but it was the boys bringing the gown.

'Then, still in the bathroom, I heard another knock. Peter let one of the boys go to the door. I hear whispering. Then I hear a shot. I run into the room. The boys have gone.

'He was there. That boy. You know the one I mean.

'He had a gun and Peter was struggling with him. There was blood streaming down Peter's head. I tried to get him away from Peter and then I felt the gun pressing into my stomach.

'He said: "Tell him to get out or I'll pull the trigger".

'I told Peter: "Peter he's got the gun at me. I can't do anything. Will you please go.' He went out and took a towel to wrap around his head. Then this boy lifts a chest of drawers and pushes it against the door. Then he put my big trunk there and chairs and goodness knows what.

'He made me get on the phone and tell his mother he was there and that he was going to kill me. She laughed and he grabbed the phone and spoke. I don't know what his mother said. Maybe she laughed at him too, but he fired into the telephone and it shattered all over the place.

'By this time Peter has got the police. I hear a dog barking and detectives are shouting through the door "Let the girl out of there" and they get the people out of the room opposite so that they can go in there and see into my room through the window.

'He kept making me play records and I did to try to calm him down. He wants a drink and all I've got is a liqueur whisky. He spat it out and sat on the bed fiddling with the gun.

'Then he got up and pointed it at my head. He says "Kiss me". I said "I won't". He said "I'll pull the trigger". I said "I don't care".

'He pulls the trigger and I faint. I either fell to the floor or fell against him or something. The gun didn't go off because while he was fiddling with the chamber he had put it where there wasn't a bullet.

'He said "Now will you kiss me?" So then I kissed him. The police must have been watching everything through the window.

'By this time his father arrives. His father shouted "It's all her fault. She's not worth bothering with. Come out son. She's not worth the trouble.'

'This made him mad. He fired through the door. He was sitting down, but he kept jerking up his gun, the sort of thing you see on television, in films. I just couldn't believe it was happening to me.

'He made me undress. He started pointing the gun at my head so I started to take off my clothes. I thought "Goodness, who's peeping in?"

'He'd drawn the curtains but I knew that people were still trying to see in if they could. I tried to stall for time, offering him another drink and putting records on, but he still wanted me to undress.

'I took off my sweater and skirt and I was in bra and pants. That wasn't enough, he wanted the whole lot off.

'So I took the whole lot off. He pushed me on the bed and started kissing me. It was all quiet and I thought he would go all the way.

'Suddenly there was a banging on the door. A detective must have got worried about the quietness in the room. This made him jump and took his mind off everything. He pointed the gun and fired at the door.

'By now I am hysterical and I'm pleading with him, practically on my hands and knees begging him to let me go. This is after two hours and suddenly he says: "Do you want to go?"

'I said "Yes" and he shouted "Hey, you out there. Are you still there? I'm going to let her go! I don't want to see you when I open the door. You'd better all get out of my sight. If I see you, I'll fire. And I'll kill her, too!"

'The police shouted: "Alright, you won't see us. We'll go."

'I was frantic in case he changed his mind. I stood waiting and said "Can I get dressed?" He said "Yes".

'I didn't dare fiddle around with underwear. I just put on my skirt and sweater. He started to pull the things away from the door and I'm praying that nobody will utter a word. He opens the door and pushes me out.

'I just collapse. Somebody picked me up and I remember seeing Peter with a towel round his head. They put me to bed but I didn't sleep. A doctor gave me an injection and I heard them say that they had got the boy out and he had fired into his own leg.

'A man from Scotland Yard came in and he wanted a statement. Next morning a reporter came and said he had seen everything through the window.'

Shirley was silent for a moment. Then she looked at me and said: 'And I was in the nude. Do you think that's what he meant by everything?'

Our stay in Australia was, in a way, the calm before the storm. Still weak and ill, I had to spend half of each day in bed, so Shirley and I did not have enough time together to clash in any serious way. She was being kept very busy with her romance with Bruce and when Bruce was not around she was having an affair with a good-looking layabout called Peter.

It was this second affair that was to prove disastrous for Shirley – and it nearly lead to her death.

But for the six months we were in Australia life was tolerably good. We had a lot of fun and Shirley reached her twenty-first birthday in Sydney. With all the force of her new adult status she put in a further claim for a white Jaguar. Unable to fight this any longer I gave in.

Tact is not a quality which features very large in Miss Bassey's make-up and when she came across a small social problem at a Christmas party in Sydney she dealt with it in true Bassey style.

Bruce Gordon was making great play with a cigarette lighter that had been given to him by a dancer billed as 'Margot the Z-Bomb'. On the lighter there was a figure of

Margot in a provocative pose.

Shirley signalled to me to get hold of the lighter, so I asked Bruce to let me examine it. As he passed it to me she grabbed it and ran to a window. Some party-goers were on their way home in the street below and she called: 'Hey, you down there. Here's a present. Merry Christmas.' She threw the lighter down.

All of this was because she had just bought Bruce a lighter she was going to give him on Christmas Day.

Towards midnight at this party, among all the champagne gaiety, Shirley became tearful.

'Oh Mickey,' she wept, 'this is the first time I've not been at home with the family for Christmas. I've always had a pillowcase full of presents at the bottom of my bed.'

At first, coming from a twenty-one-year-old in these sophisticated surroundings, I found this funny. Then I saw that she was seriously homesick and realised I would have to do something about it.

In the middle of the night I set out with Lily, who was in the same show as Shirley and with whom I was now living, to track down a Santa Claus outfit. We finally found a scruffy costumiers in a side street, woke the owner in the flat above the shop and got what we wanted.

At daylight I knocked on the lounge door of Shirley's hotel suite. She had to leave her bed and come through the lounge to answer it. As she did she saw the door from the corridor to the bedroom open and a shadowy figure creep in. Shirley rushed for her bed, screamed and pulled the sheet over her head.

The figure was Lily, in Santa suit and gumboots carrying the presents we had already bought for Shirley in a hotel pillowslip.

The Christmas Day temperature in Sydney was about a hundred in the shade and it took Lily half the day to cool off.

One cloud that nearly blacked out the Australian sunshine for us blew across the world from London and a newspaper, the Daily Sketch.

Shirley came to see me one day and said that the Sydney correspondent of the paper had called to see her and asked her if she could be in her hotel suite at a certain time to take a call from a Sketch reporter in London.

'What's the story?' I asked her.

'I don't know. Something about how I am enjoying the trip to Australia.'

I was vaguely uneasy, wondering why this could not have been dealt with by the local man, but when the call did not come at the arranged time I forgot about it and went to a cinema for an afternoon show.

Half way through the main film my name was flashed on the screen with a request for me to go immediately to the Tivoli Theatre, where Shirley was appearing in an afternoon show.

At the Tivoli I found her in hysterics. Other people in the show told me that she had started her act but had broken down in tears in the middle of a song.

I got Shirley back to her hotel, calmed her and asked for an explanation.

The Daily Sketch had called, in the middle of the night and told Shirley that they knew all about her illegitimate daughter, had a copy of the child's birth certificate and were going to publish the story on Monday – two days away.

In those less liberated days of the late Nineteen Fifties this sort of publicity could damage an entertainer's career. Plenty of people have managed to live through exposure of this sort, but I could not take the chance for Shirley.

I telephoned an old newspaper friend, Arthur Helliwell, who had a Sunday paper column, and offered him an exclusive story with a full interview with Shirley about the child if he would treat it sympathetically.

He agreed and his column that Sunday killed what would surely have been a much harsher story in the Sketch the following day.

Our skeleton was out of the cupboard and now I had to prevent it rattling too loudly. I arranged for Shirley to tell her version to an Australian magazine which responded splendidly with a 'Give Her A Break' headline and an appropriate story.

The warm-hearted Australians gave the girl all the support she could have hoped for. She got a tremendous reception at her next show and even officials in Australia seemed to ignore the business of the baby by inviting Shirley and I to a garden party for the Queen Mother a month later.

Here the star turned to a fan. Shirley was determined to meet the Queen Mother who was walking around accompanied by an official whom Shirley had got to know quite well. Occasionally the Queen Mother would stop and talk to people he introduced.

Shirley stood at the front of her row, confident of an introduction while I was well positioned opposite with a movie camera.

As the Queen Mother drew level there was a surge in the crowd and Shirley was pushed to the back by a rush of Australian royalists. I waved the camera and shouted 'Shirley, where are you?' All I could see of her was one raised eyebrow – and by then the Queen Mother had walked on.

The time for us to return to Britain was approaching and I knew that I had a tough battle ahead: partly because of the shooting incident in London, partly because of the baby revelation and partly because we had stayed in Australia just a bit too long.

Somehow I had to re-establish Shirley in Britain. I was working on that when a new little drama cropped up.

Shirley was taken ill in Melbourne with appendix trouble. She saw a doctor who treated her and advised her to take life quietly and not to go swimming.

We were due to leave within a few days and Shirley, Lily and I had decided to return by Honolulu and San Francisco. The idea was to have a few days on the beach in Hawaii and for me to drop in to Hollywood for talks with agents about future work for Shirley.

In Honolulu it was hot and I realised how annoyed Shirley would be if Lily and I were splashing in the waves while she sat it out in the sun, so I said: 'I'll make a deal with you,

Shirley. You don't want to do anything that will make you ill. We'll all go on the beach, but if you keep out of the sea, so shall I.'

For two days we lay on the beach in front of the Reef Hotel, cooking and gazing longingly at the cool water only yards away.

On the second afternoon Shirley asked: 'Do you mean that you are really not going into the sea, or that you are just waiting until I've gone into the hotel?'

'A deal's a deal,' I declared stoutly. 'I'm not going in and if I can stay out, so can you.'

'I think I'll go upstairs and lie down for a while,' said Shirley. 'I'm too hot here.'

My medical orders were to limit my time in the sun and about half an hour later I headed for the hotel, passing the swimming pool on the way.

There in the pool was the golden brown shape of Miss Bassey!

'Get out of there!' I yelled. 'You cheat. You rotten cheat.'

She giggled. I dived in. A deal's a deal.

That night I was sipping a drink on the verandah of my room when I heard a tapping sound on the other side of the partition. Shirley's room was there and I called: 'What's your trouble now?'

'Oh Mickey,' I heard. 'You had better come round. I'm not well.'

I found her twisted with pain and thinking it might be simply stomach cramps from the swimming I gave her three sleeping pills. An hour later she called again and I went to her room. She was sweating, crying and obviously in great pain. I got the hotel reception desk to call a doctor and waited with Shirley.

He came quickly. He was the most handsome sun-tanned doctor I had ever seen and, knowing Shirley, one good look at him would probably be enough to dispel her pains.

His soothing words, some simple treatment and his looks made her forget the pain for a while but the following morning at his clinic he told Shirley she must see a specialist as soon as she reached England.

On the day we left for San Francisco Shirley and I had a flaming row over money because she had overspent and did not have enough money to cover her hotel bill. We were on a restricted dollar allowance and I refused to give her any.

The result of the row was that we left the hotel separately, but before I packed I left an envelope in her key slot with a hundred dollars inside.

When I went to settle my own bill I walked over and asked the key clerk: 'Has Miss Bassey taken the envelope?'

'No sir. She's checked out and gone to the airport.'

I retrieved my envelope and left for the plane with Lily, thinking that Shirley must have paid her bill and gone away feeling too independent to take money from me.

In the plane we did not talk and at San Francisco Airport Lily and I left the plane first. As we did an airline official approached Lily:

'Are you Miss Bassey?'

'I'm her manager,' I said. 'Miss Bassey is just coming along.'

'We have had a cable from Honolulu to say that she left the Reef Hotel without paying her bill,' he said.

I pointed the man in Shirley's direction and walked to the baggage area. A few minutes later he was at my side again.

'Miss Bassey says you will pay her bill,' he said.

I turned angrily. 'You can tell Miss Bassey that I am not paying her bill. I'm going and I don't want to see her.'

I did not see Shirley again until I returned, a couple of weeks later, to London. I learned afterwards that in San Francisco she had arranged to pay the hotel bill through her bank in London, then followed us to our hotel and scraped up enough money to pay for a room for one night. The next day she caught a flight to London and as she left the hotel she wrote a farewell note for me. It said:

'I hope you're feeling happy with what you've done. May God forgive you, because I never will.'

At the time I did not know that the pains she had suffered in Hawaii had returned in San Francisco, but I was concerned enough about her health to cable a business colleague,

Leonard Beresford Clark, telling him that Shirley had been ill and asking him to look after her.

He met her at London Airport and took her to his home in Reigate, Surrey, where he and his wife looked after her for a month. Specialists attended her and the pains receded.

My plan had been for Shirley and I to arrive together at London Airport where Press cameras could record her wide-eyed delight at finding a white Jaguar tied with a big pink ribbon. That would have stamped home the fact that Shirley was back.

Instead, by the time I got back, we were just a pair of querulous invalids, divided by anger when our joint future depended upon a united front against whatever hostility might be lurking in Britain.

She got the Jaguar... unwrapped... and our first meeting was a cold little affair confined only to business topics.

Shirley was contracted to appear in a summer show on Blackpool's South Pier and before this Leslie Grade wanted her for a tour of variety theatres, opening at the Chiswick Empire. As I discussed terms with Leslie I promised him that I would get some sort of a story in the newspapers reminding a forgetful nation that Shirley Bassey still existed.

I decided that the best thing I could do to get Bassey on the front pages again would be to lose her.

We met in London and I told Shirley that she should go into hiding while I did my best to whip up a nation-wide hue and cry for the missing singer.

'That's ridiculous, Mickey,' she said. 'How can I disappear? I'm too conspicuous.'

'You're not the only coloured girl in Britain,' I grinned. 'Wear smart clothes for a change and you'll never be recognised.'

I thought she was going to give me a coloured eye for that wisecrack, so I hurried on: 'Seriously, this is the only way of getting you all over the papers right now. You've been away a long time and if we don't whip us good business at Chiswick the bookers won't want to know you and you'll be back where you started.'

'What about the numbers I'm rehearsing?'

'We'll put the piano accompaniment on tape and you can play them over wherever you are staying.'

With great reluctance Shirley agreed to disappear and we arranged to meet a few days later in the bar of the Mapleton Hotel.

In the Mapleton bar there were four people, Shirley, myself, Shirley's secretary David Gilmour and Mrs Joan Pound. Joan had been my first sweetheart and at the age of eleven I used to cycle past her home in the hope that she would look through the window. Now I needed somebody I could trust implicitly and I could think of nobody better. Joan agreed to go away with Shirley and keep her out of sight. Also she could telephone me regularly without raising suspicion.

I decided that Bath was a quiet, unsuspecting town and the last place anybody would think of associating with Bassey. At the same time it was handy for a quick return to London. My idea was for Shirley and Joan to go there by train and I walked over to the hall porter's desk at the Hotel and asked for a railway guide.

Instead of handing it over the man politely asked if he could look up anything for me. 'Yes please, I'd like the train times to Bath,' I said.

Clever, big mouth Sullivan.

In the middle of the week before the Chiswick opening two quietly dressed women took the train from Paddington station, London to Bath and a little over two hours later there checked into a quiet hotel.

I let two days pass and on a Saturday morning I walked to London's West End Central police station and spoke to the duty sergeant.

He hauled me over to a detective and in a waiting room with dirty walls and furnished with a table and two upright wooden chairs I was asked:

'What can I do for you sir?'

I tried to look worried, but not uncomfortable. 'My name is Sullivan – Michael Sullivan. I'm personal manager to Miss Shirley Bassey. I think she's missing.'

'Oh? What gives you that impression?'

I explained that Shirley had failed to keep an appointment two days ago for a rehearsal and that she had not been seen at her hotel.

'Since then I haven't heard from her and I can find nobody who has.'

I added that she might have gone to her mother's home in Cardiff, but was sure that she would have told me if she had.

'There are only two days to go before she opens a show at Chiswick and she always turns up for rehearsals.' I said.

The detective took a note of Shirley's mother's address and then asked:

'Did you have an argument or anything that would make her not want to see you?'

I shrugged. 'Yes, we had a bitter argument, but that's nothing new. We're always having rows. I suppose we are both pretty temperamental. But she's always turned up for rehearsals.'

The detective asked me to leave the matter with him for a few hours and telephone him that afternoon.

I thanked him and left and later I called him. He had checked with Cardiff and Shirley was not there and had not been there.

I said: 'You are beginning to panic me a little now. You know there was some unpleasantness with a gun before this girl left for Australia?'

He vaguely remembered and this helped to convince him that I was genuinely worried.

'We'll put her on the missing persons list,' he said. 'Have you a picture of her we could have?'

I had about a thousand, but I had been waiting for him to suggest this and then I asked the all-important question:

'Do you think,' I said in a small voice, 'we ought to give it out to the Press? After all, she's a public personality. Somebody might have seen her.'

'I don't see why not.'

'Do you think it would be better if you did it? I'm not sure of the best thing to do...'

'I'll deal with it,' said the helpful policeman, which was just what I was praying for. I wanted this stunt to be as official as I could make it.

I was staying at Airways Mansions, in Haymarket, and I sat in my room and suffered an invasion. Night and day from Saturday evening until Monday morning there were reporters with me and the telephone rang every few minutes.

They questioned me and hounded me and tried to beat me down. 'Come on Mike, come clean,' said those who knew me well, but I held out.

On the Saturday evening Shirley's 'disappearance' was on TV news, with her picture, and the story made the Sunday papers – and big. Now everyone knew Bassey was back in Britain... but where?

Ironically, it was the Daily Sketch – thwarted by me over the baby story in Australia – which got on to the truth. A Sketch reporter called Jack Lewis came to tell me that he knew Shirley was in Bath. I denied it, but he told me he had questioned the porter at the Mapleton who had recalled looking up the Bath train times for me.

I tried to bluff my way out but the following day the paper carried a story which indicated I had admitted everything. I had not, but after Australia I had to grant them some licence and we were now pegging level.

Despite the story that morning I carried the bluff through Monday – until the moment Shirley arrived in time for her first show at Chiswick Empire saying: 'Me missing? I just went away for a rest.'

I could see the story rounding itself off nicely in the Tuesday newspapers – but before the night was over there was a very different Bassey story for the morning.

As Shirley started her second song an egg hurtled down from the gallery of the theatre. It smashed on the stage just behind her and did not affect her singing in the slightest. She just saw a white form flash by her and thought somebody had thrown a flower.

We never caught the youth who threw the egg and the next day a 'Bassey pelted with eggs' story was the current chapter of the saga.

Anybody who says 'No publicity is bad' is an idiot. That one egg was a disaster. It ruined the effect I had carefully built up over Shirley's disappearance and it kept people away from the theatre. On Monday the takings at Chiswick were four hundred pounds. Through the week they dropped to one hundred, seventy and, finally, to sixty.

People put on their best clothes for the theatre and they don't want to risk getting in the way of an egg, even if it is meant for somebody else.

Naturally, after the Daily Sketch story of the 'disappearance' I was called to West End Central police station.

Another detective – a higher ranking one this time – told me: 'This is a serious matter and I must caution you Mister Sullivan. We are concerned with the fact that you may have been using the police to your own advantage. We are not sure whether you have done so or not, but I wish to place on record that I am warning you against ever doing it or trying it.'

I spluttered a denial, but thanked him for the warning and left, trying not to look too guilty.

The second week of Shirley's variety tour took her to Birmingham and it was here that the pains in her side returned. By two in the morning she was in hospital, and a doctor was on the telephone to me in London.

I was cynical. 'Look,' I said. 'Somebody threw an egg at her last week. Business went to pot and now she doesn't feel like facing another bad week. That's all that's wrong with her.'

'No Mister Sullivan,' the doctor said. 'It's something much more serious. I have a consultant coming in. Ring me back in an hour.'

I sweated out the hour and when I called the hospital I was told she had peritonitis and an immediate operation was vital. Without it she could die and even with it there was no guarantee.

The operation went ahead and for a time Shirley was on the danger list. She was unable to work for six weeks. Leslie Grade called off the variety tour and James Brennan, who had booked her for the South Pier show in Blackpool agreed to cancel the contract. We were both relieved to get out of our obligations because the advance bookings for it were negligible. That Chiswick egg was still sending up a stink.

Scene Five: Shirley Bassey's Marriage

When Shirley was fully recovered I found that nobody was keen to book her. The only way to get her started again was to back her bills with my own money. The mid-summer doldrums had hit the Moss Empires theatre circuit and they welcomed my offer to put in a show to tour their circuit.

Shirley sang as well as ever on that tour, but the telephone was silent. I had to find a way to start it ringing again.

The biggest event in British show business that summer was a charity show by Sir Laurence Olivier, 'The Night Of A Hundred Stars'. I dialled the number of the organiser and said:

'I notice that Miss Shirley Bassey has not been invited to appear on your show even though she is prepared to give her services. Am I to assume that there is some colour prejudice?'

'No of course there's not,' the organiser assured me. 'I'll call you back.'

This was pure blackmail on my part. I was gambling on my infamous reputation of rushing to the newspapers with any story that I thought would raise some dust and I knew that no reputable body would like to be tainted with the cry of 'colour bar'.

Ten minutes later my telephone rang and Shirley was on the show.

She stole the show and every booker in the audience was clapping his little red hands. The next day my silent telephone got its voice back.

Shirley herself was responsible for our next stroke of luck. Johnny Franz wanted her to record a ballad called 'Hands

Across The Sea' and said to her: 'All we want now is a good song for the B side.'

Shirley found another ballad called 'As I Love You' and dashed to telephone Franz.

'Johnny, I've got a song. It has this middle eight which is ME. I can change key and HIT... attack it! It's just...'

'What's it called', Johnny asked.

'As I Love You.'

'I've got it here and I've played it over. It's another ballad. We don't want two ballads. We want something with a beat.'

But Shirley kept calling Johnny and after two weeks he gave in.

Because she liked the song Shirley put everything she knew into it. At the same time she recorded another song 'Kiss Me Honey, Honey Kiss Me' and for three months the two numbers chased each other around the Hit Parade, passing and re-passing like a couple of six-day bike riders.

To help the race along I insisted that Shirley sang one of these two songs on every radio or TV show I accepted for her. But this lead to disagreement between us.

Shirley was due to sing 'Kiss Me Honey' on a show and during rehearsals her musical director called me: 'She says she's fed up singing "Kiss Me Honey", Mike. She insists on doing "As I Love You"'.

I was ill in bed at the time, but even flat on my back I considered myself a match for Miss Bassey.

'Okay,' I said. 'Tell her she's singing "As I Love You". But take the music for "Kiss Me Honey". Then what can she do?'

She sang "Kiss Me Honey".

To me it was another small victory. To Shirley it was one more cause for resentment.

Shirley was right back on top with two songs in the Top Ten and ready to star in 'Blue Magic' a revue at London's Prince of Wales Theatre which was destined to run for months.

All was well with the world... and she was about to ditch me.

I thought she ought to exercise some of her new songs for

'Blue Magic' before the show opened and booked her into a variety bill at Colchester, Essex. Twice during her week there I went to Colchester to discuss business with her. Each time there were two men in her dressing room, two young West End 'faces' who ran a drinking club in Soho – Clive Sharp and Maurice King. I wanted to speak to her privately but she said: 'It's perfectly all right, anything you wish to say can be said in front of these gentlemen.'

Clive Sharp and I had met before, when Shirley brought him to a Christmas dinner at my home. To me he was just another boy friend, but he saw himself playing a role in her business life as well as her romantic one. Clive Sharp was, softly and quietly, taking her from me.

Back in London the time came for rehearsals for 'Blue Magic'. Shirley did not turn up on the Monday, nor on the Tuesday. She was living then in a flat in the Thameside block Dolphin Square and I went to see her on the Tuesday evening.

She gave it to me absolutely straight: She thought I had been taking too much money from her and that a normal manager was entitled to only twenty per cent of her earnings.

'I'll go along with that', I said. 'Twenty per cent will suit me fine, so long as I no longer have to pay out for agents' commissions, fares, new music, costumes, flowers, hire of jewellery, entertainment and all the other things I have been finding money for.'

We agreed to tear up our old contracts and sign new ones. I phoned our solicitor – the same man was acting for both of us – and asked him to arrange a new contract between Shirley and James Bauries, the producer of 'Blue Magic'; to terminate my contract with Shirley and draw up a new one under which I would receive twenty per cent of her earnings.

The new contract between Shirley and Laurie was issued the next say and my original contract was torn up.

Then Shirley told me I was finished!

She said that her two new advisers, Sharp and King had told her that I had cheated her out of her share of the Colchester show, which incidentally made a loss. I said I would sue her. She said our original contract had been illegal all along.

It did not matter what we said.

The only important thing was: Bassey and Sullivan were washed up.

Within days Shirley had two new managers – Clive Sharp and Maurice King, would you believe? She had a new agent too, and one of the first things the new manager Clive did was to ban me from the back stage area of the Prince Of Wales. But he could not stop me taking a seat in the stalls for the opening night.

For two years I walked around with a Bassey-shaped hole in my heart – and in my pocket. I was suing her for eight thousand pounds, tax free, and could not act as anyone else's manager because of my exclusive contract with Shirley, which I was attempting to prove was still in force.

For a while I ran a strip club in St James's – the London locality better known for clubs of a much more sedate style – and dabbled in show business where I could.

Friends had tried to console me by saing: 'You'll see Mike, one day she'll call you and ask you to come back.'

I did not believe them. Until one o'clock on a cold December morning when my bedside telephone jangled me into consciousness.

I groped for the handset and dragged it beneath the blankets. A small tentative voice said: 'Mike?' giving the vowel sound two syllables, one high and one low, musically about a fourth apart. 'Mi-ike.'

'Yes?'   'It's me.'

Christmas was still two weeks away. It was closed season for guessing games.

'Who's me?'

'Shirley.'

'Shirley who?'

The angry yell that came over the telephone almost jerked me out of bed.

'Don't tell me you don't know who Shirley is! How many other Shirleys have you made into a star?' She said it 'Staaah', all on one long, hard, bright note that only needed a backing of muted brass.

'Oh, that Shirley. What do you want?' 'I want to see you.'

'When?'

'Tomorrow.'

The court case between us was set for January 8 and it was now December 14. This could be a plot to talk me out of going ahead with what I considered to be a very strong case. I decided to play hard to get.

'Can't make it tomorrow. Make it the day after.' Not TOO hard to get.

'Six o'clock then?'

'Right.' We put down the telephones.

Later I called my lawyer. He saw no problem with us meeting, providing we opened the proceedings with the declaration 'without prejudice'.

A 'bing-bong' version of her hit song 'As I Love You' chimed out as I pressed the front door button to the narrow terraced house just a few yards from Hyde Park.

Gerda, the German housekeeper, opened the door and I forced my feet through the deep pile of red carpeting which covered the hallway and the stairs until I reached the first landing.

Shirley stood at the door of the first-floor sitting room wearing an ankle-length brown velvet robe and a haughty, man-eating expression which she subconsciously puts on to face any new or uncomfortable experience.

The haughtiness melted as I reached the doorway. Her arms opened and she hugged me. Feeling very foolish I said: 'Without prejudice.' She laughed. 'Oh yes, without prejudice.'

I am sure that neither of us knew exactly what that phrase meant, but for a moment it gave us a warm, secure feeling – the way a child about to tell a white lie when he had his fingers crossed behind his back.

We sat five yards apart and for ten minutes we hedged. Then I said: 'Look, let's stop all the humming and hawing. What is all this about?'

It came out in a flood.

'Mickey,' she said, 'you always treated me like a child. Like a freak. You arranged things without telling me and I only used to find out about them when somebody else told me or I read about them somewhere.

'I know now that you were trying to save me from disappointment if things didn't materialise, but at the time I used to think you were doing things behind my back.

'People said to me "He's deceiving you" and I believed them. They said "You're the star. He only works for you".'

Shirley went on to explain how much she had enjoyed her freedom after she had kicked me out – arranging her own bookings; making her own professional decisions about gowns and music.

For her, that first year away from me had been wonderful.

But since then, with nobody around strong enough to pull the strings, she had become bored... and lazy. She also missed the luxury of an exclusive management. 'I need somebody to look after me alone,' she said. 'Somebody who thinks I am enough.'

'In other words, Mickey, I want you back.'

I sat back and closed my eyes. I kept them tight shut while I told her of the friends who had said: 'One day she'll call you and ask you to come back.'

Then I opened my eyes, went over to the wide, rust-coloured chair she was sitting in and we hugged each other. In a pleading little voice she asked: 'Will you help me?'

For my part the emotion lasted all of two good, sentimental minutes. Then the agent took over.

'Shirley, has somebody put you up to this?'

'No Mickey. I just thought of it lying in bed. Probably all this year it has been at the back of my mind and suddenly it came to the front.'

I tried to think calmly about her offer. Shirley Bassey, the singer, was my creation and I badly wanted her back, to guide her career and carry her forward to the place I had always had in mind for her among the top stars in the world. On the other hand she had been a damned nuisance. Looking after her had wrecked my health once and could easily do so again.

I told her some of this and she swore she had changed, that she was more placid, more sensible, more mature. She seemed to be telling the truth.

'We won't say any more tonight Shirley,' I said. 'Join me for dinner.'

That night she ate and I drank. In a premature kind of way, I was celebrating.

It took a week – including a dramatic walk out on my part from a meeting with her agent Jock Jacobson – and a lot of heart searching on both sides before Shirley and I got together in Wolverhampton one rainy, cold night and came to terms for renewing the partnership.

I dropped my claim for eight thousand pounds tax free to six thousand and of this one third was to be taken from commission earned under our new agreement, but Shirley would pay the tax on it.

As her manager once more I received twenty per cent of all of her earnings and she paid her own expenses.

We signed the deal at her solicitor's office. She turned up ten minutes late for the meeting, signed the contract without reading a line of it, kissed me and breezed out.

Within three weeks Shirley and I were back in Australia and it was here that she showed that those two years in which she had been the mistress of her own affairs had left their mark.

During one late night show at the club where she was appearing she totally lost control. For more than a month she had been singing to appreciative and attentive audience, but on this night one party in the room talked loudly throughout her act.

Shirley was seething and at the end of her second song she wanted to walk off. But the entertainer took the upper hand and she persevered. Her final song 'The Party's Over' was very dramatic and she knew that the chatter would kill it stone dead.

When she came to the end of the song before it she said to the musical director 'Play me off' and left the stage.

I doubt if anybody in the audience knew they had been cheated out of a song – but I saw red.

I barged into the curtained alcove that served as her dressing room.

'Don't you dare come in!' yelled Shirley. 'I'm undressed.' In fact, she was wrapped in a big towel.

'I don't care. Want to talk to you. I don't care if you are the Queen of England, you don't walk out on an audience.'

Shirley blazed: 'What the hell are you talking about. If I had walked off in the middle of a number you would have something to complain about. For all they know I finished my act. You have no argument. The only time I can do what I want is when I am on that stage. Then I'm the boss. So get out!'

And then she kicked me, barefoot, on the rear as I turned to walk out on her.

Our argument continued afterwards at a table in the club and then she announced: 'I'm going to have a little drink.'

She had more than one little drink and I left her to them and went to bed.

Full of boozy bravado Miss Bassey decided to keep the battle going. Throughout the night she woke me by telephoning and asking: 'Have you packed yet? I suppose you are taking the next plane out?' and 'Hello, are you getting a good night's sleep?'

After the first four calls I gave up trying to sleep and lay there, waiting for the next round.

One thing was certain: We had come a long way from the days when I controlled a puppet called Shirley Bassey, an unsure little girl who used to do everything I told her, whose only answer was 'Yes, Mr Sullivan.'

A long, long way.

We papered over our quarrel and on the way home after two months in Australia we decided to stop off for a few days in New York.

There took place a meeting that was to develop into one of the most tragic periods of Shirley's life.

We had been in our hotel only a few hours when she came

to me and said: 'Guess who's here? Kenny Hume.'

At the time I was negotiating for Shirley to appear in a six week season at the Opera House, Blackpool for impresario George Black, who was also staying at the hotel, and I took little notice. Kenneth Hume was a TV commercial director I had seen around in London. He was homosexual, full of charm, two-faced and thoroughly detestable. Shirley's remark about him being at the hotel was at the time, nothing more to me than a passing remark.

In any case, I would have seen nothing wrong in Shirley talking to him. Somebody with his sexual proclivities couldn't pose any threat to a healthy, lusty girl like her. Shirley always liked her men masculine.

I should have taken more notice. By our fourth day in the hotel Hume was actively courting Shirley and she was lapping up all the fawning attention he was paying to her.

Back home in London I heard no more of Hume until late one evening I was telephoned by John Mills, the owner of Les Ambassadeurs, a very luxurious club on Park Lane, who told me that Shirley was there and had just announced her engagement to Kenneth Hume.

I asked John to send them a bottle of champagne with my congratulations and went back to sleep.

The following day Hume turned up at a concert in Leicester with Shirley in a gleaming hired Rolls Royce. The matter was now becoming serious. He was getting his claws in and to me it was a case of her money, not her love, that he wanted.

I tried to talk Shirley out of the whole sorry affair:

'Look, it can't work. He's queer. How can you want somebody like that. You're a healthy, sexy girl. Go and find somebody who can give you what you really want. Jump into bed with them and get him out of your system.'

It did not work. Shirley was really in love with Hume, she was convinced she could change him and wanted to marry.

I dared not argue any more with her. All I could do was pray that she would come to her senses.

She did not and they married.

'I know he's queer,' she told me. 'But, Mickey, all that will change. You wait and see.'

I waited and the next thing I saw was their arrival in the South of France for the Cannes film festival. Shirley and Hume were living in great style at the Carlton, the most expensive hotel in the town, and one night at a casino in Juan Les Pins, near Cannes, I watched him playing three roulette tables at the same time.

'Mike, he CAN gamble,' John Mills had told me. And he could.

Hume's gradual annexation of Shirley's professional as well as her private life was in classic style. He had a company into which all of her earnings went, he developed a taste for Rolls Royces and he then started a war of nerves against me.

Part of his campaign was to tell me that I should be standing in the wings holding a glass of water and toilet tissues for Shirley at every performance.

He might just as well have asked me to go on stage and do her act myself. My response to his demand that I became Shirley's skivvy was just two words. The second of them was 'off'.

While Shirley was working in Blackpool I received a letter from Hume telling me that I was in breach of my contract with her. I went north to the Opera House and in Shirley's dressing room Hume told me that he did not want me to go with them when Shirley appeared in New York later that year.

'I cannot stand any more of this aggravation from you,' I told Hume. 'The best thing you can do is to buy me out.'

I took a cheque for ten thousand pounds and – for the second time – the Bassey-Sullivan partnership was at an end.

Shortly after our parting Shirley came running back to me.

Early one evening I took a telephone call from her home in Maida Vale, West London. She was hysterical and distraught. She had caught Hume in bed, making love to her chauffeur.

I was working from my home, just over a mile away at

Regents Park and told her to come to me immediately.

Shirley almost fell out of the taxi that stopped outside my flat. She was in a terrible state, screaming, sobbing and shaking, and I took her in and tried to comfort her. It was no good telling her 'I told you so', all I could do was cuddle her and let her pour her heart out to me.

'Mickey, I really thought that he was out of all that,' she croaked. 'How could he?'

I was about to tell her how he could, how leopards don't change their spots, or homosexuals their choice of bed-mates when Hume arrived at the flat.

He, too, was in tears and there was nothing I could do with two weeping people both trying to use me as a sounding board and peacemaker. I called a taxi for Shirley, told her to go home and wait to hear from me.

'You and I,' I told Hume, 'had better have a talk. Sit down.'

He burst into more tears and slumped into a chair.

'Ken, I don't like you and you don't like me,' I said. 'But that is of no consequence. I like Shirley. In spite of all of our troubles I love her like a daughter and I will not allow something like you to upset her.

'I can't tell her to kick you out because that will make me look vindictive. But I can tell you this: Those tears are either crocodile or real.

'I pray, for your sake that they are real, because although Shirley and I may not be friends I will always be on call if she needs me. And if she does call me and you are the cause of the trouble I will break your fucking neck. Understand?'

Hume could do nothing more than nod... and start crying again.

'I'm telling you now to go home to Shirley. When you have left I am going to call her and tell her to take you in her arms and try to start again.'

Hume left and, for a while, it seemed, as though they had repaired their marriage. But it was not to last and not long after they parted for good the pathetic Ken Hume committed suicide.

At the time of the incident with the chauffeur I am sure that

Shirley and I could have got together for a third time, but I had established myself as a director of the powerful Bernard Delfont Agency and I could not risk having Shirley Bassey as part of my life again.

Twice bitten is enough for any man... even me.

ACT FOUR
Scene One: My Five Wives

No man in his right senses should ever have as many wives as I have had. But then, no man in his right senses would ever choose to be a theatrical agent for a living, and as show business and beautiful women are so inextricably locked together I suppose it was only natural that I should take advantage of whatever came my way. I have loved, lost and cheated on a full handful of wives and countless girl friends. I have had offers I couldn't refuse from beautiful girls anxious to break into show business and I have made more than a few offers myself.

But one offer I not only turned down but ran away from came from one of the most beautiful stars ever to appear on the screen, the late Vivien Leigh.

Had I been all grown up and mature things would have been different, but I met the gorgeous, glamorous Vivien when I was just eighteen years old.

In my very early days as an agent I had booked a skating act for a film being made by Paramount at Elstree Studios, a few miles from London, and – as a dutiful agent – I had gone to the studios to ensure that everything was going well. Vivien Leigh was there at the time and I was honoured at being introduced to her... the first time I had got up close to a real big movie star.

She was leaving Elstree to return to London and offered me a lift in her chauffeured car. Nervously, I accepted and tried to make pleasant small talk on the journey.

When we arrived at her flat in Piccadilly she asked me if I would like to come up to the apartment for a drink. I accepted mainly because I wanted to see the sort of style the great lady lived in.

Once in the apartment she poured me a whisky and soda and then left the room. 'I must change into something more comfortable,' she explained.

A few minutes later she called me into her bedroom. She was sprawled on the bed wearing a pink negligee and pointed to a chair in the corner.

'Now this is what we are going to do,' she said. 'You will sit there and I will stay on the bed. I will excite myself and you will excite yourself.

'Then we will see what happens.'

I fled.

It was nearly thirty years later that we met again, this time because an old friend in the business, 'Bumble' Dawson, told me one day, 'Vivien has got T.B. She is feeling very low. Why don't you try to find a play for her to do? It would be good for both of you.'

Before I started calling for scripts I decided it would be best to meet Vivien Leigh and discuss the matter with her. Through 'Bumble' I made an appointment and travelled to her country house in Sussex. We took tea together and I was introduced to the actor she was then living with.

It was a charming way to spend an afternoon, but we never got around to agreeing on a play and I am sure she never recognised me as the frightened boy of so many years ago.

One other sexual encounter I had was nowhere near so promising. In fact it terrified the life out of me, particularly because my would-be bed partner was my boss – and a man!

After the Second World War started in September 1939 I decided – like so many other young men – that I wanted to be a fighter pilot.

I got into the Royal Air Force easily enough and was even selected for pilot training, but an administrative error ruined my chances of ever getting into the cockpit of a Spitfire. The R.A.F. admitted the error, but – in the manner of all bureaucracies – refused to set the record straight and I was sent for training as an air gunner.

This was not my idea of the way in which to fight the war, so I went home. Eventually I was recaptured, escaped and finally discharged after spending months in an R.A.F. hospital suffering from neurasthenia.

I went back to work in the theatre business, working as a booker from an office in Blackpool for a man called Hyman Zahl, one of the top London agents.

Hymie was short, stocky, bespectacled – and gay. This last quality was something I knew nothing about until I had to meet him one night in Sheffield to see a show starring two great comedians, Issy Bonn and Jimmy James.

After the show the four of us sat around drinking in the hotel lounge. I grew tired, wished the others goodnight and went to the room I was sharing with Hymie.

I woke up when I found someone in my single bed with me: Hymie, breathing heavy words of affection and trying to 'make' me!

As tactfully as I could I explained to him that I was a good Catholic boy who did not go in for that sort of thing and then spent the rest of night, tightly wrapped in the bed clothes, eyes wide open and hardly daring to breath.

That morning I went to London and formally left Hymie's employ.

By now the war was almost over and after trying to work on my own again I went back to Hymie's agency on the firm understanding that it was strictly business. Neither Hymie nor I ever held that incident in Sheffield against each other.

One of the jobs I had while working for him was booking concerts for the servicemen in Europe and for one show I needed a really good-looking girl to act as a hostess and introduce the performers.

The gorgeous Kay Kendall, who later became one of the most popular British stars of the Nineteen Fifties got the job and together we travelled by train to Germany where she would present the show.

There were four other people – all unknown to us – in the compartment. I sat quietly reading a book while Kay had buried herself in a newspaper.

I was no longer the shy boy who had run away from that

215

bedroom in Piccadilly and late during the evening I leant forward and mouthed to her: 'Shall we?'

She folded her paper, put it down and said: 'Why not?' and led me out of the compartment to the lavatory.

There, of all places, we made love – just two people who happened to be sharing the same train journey.

Kay's forthright and down-to-earth reaction to what was, after all, just a frivolous but hopeful remark of mine was typical of the girl. But I was never able to look her straight in the eye again.

According to that eminent sexologist Dr Kinsey, half of all married men cheat on their wives at least once. Should this bring outraged cries of 'Not me!' from the faithful and ever-loving, it must be considered that such statistics are usually a mean average taken from a large sample group and one man philandering a little more than the average can really bump the figures up.

In my case, I have contributed more than a normal share to Dr Kinsey's conclusion, which accounts for the fact that I am now happy with my fifth wife.

But with numbers one to four life was a game of leap-frogging from one to the other – and grabbing every available opportunity in between.

I married my first wife, Joan, when I was still in the Royal Air Force and she was a restaurant manageress in Blackpool who had been dating my best friend. That marriage lasted just over three years and a number of affairs on my side.

My second wife was also my secretary and we had never planned on marrying – just living and working together. But to keep her parents happy we trotted off to a register office.

Kit, my second wife, and I stayed together until I met Juhni Holloway, a West End stage costume designer. Once again we had no thoughts of marriage, but it became a little embarrassing going to dinners and functions attended by the top brass of show business and having no Mrs Sullivan in tow.

So Juhni and I faked a wedding!

I arrived at my office one day wearing a new suit and a carnation and ostentatiously ordered a cab to take me to

Caxton Hall at eleven a.m. This started off the gossip that I was about to wed secretly and after lunch I returned with Juhni, wearing a big hat.

The ruse worked and people were convinced that we were man and wife. Some months later I had got used to having a wife around, so Juhni and I actually did get married, although this time it was done so secretly that nobody knew about it.

Juhni and I broke up in the early days of my management of Shirley Bassey when I met Lily Berde, a tremendous Greek dancer whom I had known in Hollywood.

Romancing Lily with Juhni around was never easy and after Juhni and I had officially parted I was still a little in love with her.

Shirley was appearing in Cardiff and I had installed Lily in my hotel there ... but I still wanted Juhni.

'Why don't you come here for a few days, just for old times sake?' I asked her on a call to London. 'You never know how it could develop.'

Juhni accepted the invitation and arrived by train. I booked her into a hotel about half a mile from the one I was staying in with Lily and for the next five days I divided my time between three women.

During the day I was taking care of Shirley's business affairs and I would spend part of each night with the other two.

I used Shirley as the excuse for leaving Juhni's bed in the early hours of the morning, telling her that I had to start work at the crack of dawn and when I climbed in beside Lily I told her I had been out half the night negotiating deals.

At the end of five days I was on my knees and had privately pledged never to be so ambitious again.

Lily and I never married, but we stayed together for fourteen years and we have both always considered that we spent that time together as husband and fourth wife.

We were together when Jayne Mansfield arrived in London and I decided that to star her in a stage play of 'Forever Amber', the novel that was considered so shocking when it was first published but would now fall into the category of primary school reading, could be a money-spinning attraction.

I knew nothing of Jayne's reputation as a man-eater when I appeared at her hotel suite with a copy of the book and a list of ideas for transforming it into a play. But I soon learned.

She greeted me from a settee, wearing flimsy black underwear from which her ample charms were spilling.

'C'mon and sit down here,' she drawled, patting the space at her side. I sat.

Miss Mansfield's appreciation of literature had probably never got beyond the comic book stage and she leaned heavily over me while I delineated the more interesting passages of the book. Within twenty minutes she was almost smothering me.

Never one to turn away from a good thing, I responded and our business discussion became a full practical audition for the sexy part of Amber St Clair, right there on the settee.

'Forever Amber' was a project I never managed to present on stage. If I had, with Jayne Mansfield in the role, I doubt if I would have lasted the run of the show!

I began to cheat on Lily more and more and each time I took greater chances. The thought of what she would do with her fiery Greek temper if ever she caught me out seemed to rouse my adrenalin. I was excited and scared witless at the same time.

On one Spanish holiday with Lily I fell for a good-looking German girl whose room was three doors down the hotel corridor from ours.

Unluckily for her but fortunately for me, Lily caught 'flu and had to spend two days in bed. I dated the girl, spent the night with her and then had to face the problem of explaining to Lily my appearance in our room at five thirty in the morning.

Our hotel was built on the side of a small harbour and at dawn I crept out and jumped on a fishing boat that was just about to leave. The Spanish skipper was astounded by the appearance of this uninvited tourist and started to shout, ordering me off.

I shouted back and watched as our combined bellowing

woke guest after guest in the hotel. Lily's curtains remained closed.

I shouted more and started swearing at the man, who did not understand one word of what I said. Eventually Lily appeared at her window. She saw what was going on and yelled:

'Michael. What are you doing? Leave that man alone.'

As she did the frustrated fisherman rushed me and half carried me on to the quayside.

I stood there, faking rage, as he started his engine and chugged off and then strode into the hotel.

In our room I explained to Lily: 'That bastard. He took two thousand pesetas from me and then wouldn't keep his end of the deal.'

'What do you mean?'

'Well, you know how much I love fishing? I met this man in a bar last night and he agreed to take me out this morning. I've sat up all night waiting for him – and now this.'

Lily made all the right sympathetic noises, pushed me into the shower and then made me go to bed to recover from my all-night wait. I needed the rest.

Lilly and I began to come to an end on June 1 1966 when I boarded a Caravelle at London's Heathrow Airport for Paris.

I was flying there to try to set a deal for the rights to the World Cup film 'Goal!', based on the possession of a lot of promises, but no money.

In the departure lounge I saw a beautiful blonde woman in her thirties and I told Octavio Senoret, my partner and travelling companion: 'I've got to get to know her.'

With some careful manouevring I was seated next to her when we took off and asked her 'Do you speak English?'

She told me that she was French and that she did speak my language.

'Good. I wonder if you can help me. I am very nervous and this is the first time I have flown. What do I do with this safety belt?'

Patiently she explained it all to me and I then introduced myself.

'And what's your name?'

'Dany Robin,' she said. She pronounced it 'row-ban'.
'Dany what?'
'Robin. For you it's like robin, the little bird with the red front.'

Believing that the best way into any situation is with both feet first, I told her that I had fallen in love with her and would marry her.

'You are ridiculous,' she answered. 'I am a married woman with children.'

'Maybe, but you don't look happy. I am going to marry you. It may take two years or more. But I will.'

All she could do was laugh, but as we talked on that flight I learned that she was one of France's leading film and stage stars and had been married for years to film star George Marchall. Superficially their marriage was the most idyllic in French show business, but I later learned that it had been breaking apart for a long time.

It took me two years to woo, bed and wed Dany and during that time our courtship was carried out in her sister Coco's flat in Paris.

I flew to the French capital nearly ever week-end, but could never be seen in public with her because she was so well-known.

Sometimes Dany would come to London, but even then we could only frequent places that were not used by people in the entertainment business.

To throw her husband off the scent I became her London agent and then had an excuse for meeting her at her magnificent chateau home at Montfort Lamaury.

I took a script to Montfort Lamaury for Dany and while we were sitting alone in the drawing room George Marchall walked in. He had returned early from filming a Western in Yugoslavia. Had he got home in the evening instead of the afternoon he would certainly have found us together in another room!

One of the few people who knew of our affair was Dany's French agent, Olga Primuz. Olga, who also handled Brigitte Bardot, had a wicked sense of humour and one night when I went with her and Dany to the opening of a play in Paris we were suddenly surrounded by photographers during the interval.

I had an actor client appearing in the play, so had every valid reason for being there, but it now looked as though my secret romance was going to burst into the open.

Dany and Olga went back into the theatre while I faced the crowd.

'What do you want, gentlemen?'

One of them, who spoke excellent English, said they had been tipped off that there was a new man in Dany Robin's life. Was it me?

I thought at about twice the speed of light and laughed.

'All my life I have handled show business stars in England. I have always stood by while people have taken photographs of them. Nobody has ever shown me any attention and I am flattered that you should,' I said.

'Go ahead, where do you want me to stand for your pictures?'

Not one of them lifted a camera.

Later, over dinner, Olga admitted to Dany and I that she had tipped off the photographers. 'Just my idea of a little joke, Michael. I wanted to see how you would get out of it.'

It did take me a full two years to woo Dany and when she announced she was leaving George Marchall the news was front-paged all over the Continent.

We married in 1969 and here and now I can state categorically that there will definitely not be a sixth Mrs Sullivan.

But even our wedding day, November 23, with an attendant guard of honour of Air France hostesses to remind us both of our first meeting, very nearly did not happen.

Dany's strict Catholic conscience began to trouble her. She took her marriage vows to George very seriously... despite his many affairs during their marriage.

In public they may have been the fairy tale prince and princess of the French screen, but very soon after they married she realised that her husband was a Casanova of epic style.

A woman without her strong and almost unbending

221

morality might have gone her own way. But not Dany. In fact, only once was she inclined to rock the boat and that was when Charlie Chaplin's actor son Sidney started to pay court to her when he was living in Paris. To him it was the start of a very serious emotional involvement, but Dany just flirted a little, to teach George a lesson.

In 1968 Dany met me in Paris and told me she wanted to finish our affair. This was something I just could not live with and I telephoned an Irish friend, Nick Connors, in Dublin and asked him to find a Dominican monk who would talk to us both.

The meeting was arranged and Dany and I went to Dublin and met Father John. We took it in turn to explain our respective situations and our feeling for each other. I, for one, held nothing back and the man seemed so overwhelmed with our frankness that he gave us a blessing.

This was the emotional and spiritual cushion that Dany needed so much and the monk himself seemed so overwhelmed with our love for each other that he threw dogma to the winds and advised us to marry.

After the wedding and a reception with a guest list that read like a 'Who's Who' of show business we had a specially chartered helicopter to fly us from the Fairmile Hotel in Surrey to London's Heathrow Airport for the start of our honeymoon.

But that meeting in Dublin was not the last of Father John. Nine months after Dany and I married he came to see me in my London office to explain that he had left the Church. He had married and asked me if I could help to find a job for him in journalism. He also explained that at the time of our meeting he was already involved with a lady whom he had since married, so when we pleaded our case to him we could not have found a more sympathetic ear!

When we married Dany happily gave in to my wish that she would not work again. My business was successful and I was able to give her a beautiful home, a Rolls Royce and even a yacht for her birthday.

Even before the wedding she was determined that work

would not interfere with our plans and by sticking to her resolve she almost threw away the chance of a lifetime... to be directed by the masterful Alfred Hitchcock.

At the time I was acting as her London agent and when I got a call asking if Dany Robin was available to meet the great man I was ecstatic with excitement.

I managed to hold the news until I got home. When I did tell Dany her reaction was one of great reluctance.

Eventually I persuaded her to meet Hitchcock in Paris and she agreed only because it would give her a chance to see her family.

I met her on her return to Heathrow Airport and asked: 'What happened?'

With an air of total disinterest she explained that they had shared a beautiful lunch and Hitch had discussed his favourite subject – French wines.

'Michael, he was amazed that I was such a connoisseur.'

'Yes, yes, but what about the film?'

'Oh that. He explained the part and I told him that the filming would interfere with our wedding plans.'

'You have got to be crazy! To be directed by that man would be the crowning point of your career. We can always change the date of the wedding.'

'But I thought you wanted me to retire?'

Weeks later I had almost forgotten about the film when I received a cable offering Dany the lead part in 'Topaz'. That film kept us apart for nearly three months, but it meant that Dany bowed out of the business right at the very top.

FALSE TABS

This book would never have been written without the persistent encouragement of my sister Sheila, Des O'Connor (and I'm glad I've never encouraged him to sing), Michael Parkinson and Tom Merrin of the London Daily Mirror.

In the past few years I have undergone three major operations and each time I have been on the 'write off' list. Apart from the skill of the surgeons, it has been the courage and tenderness of my Dany that has pulled me through and enabled me to be here to finish this book.

This story may be at an end – but I'm not. I have just completed a film script 'On The Hook' and it has been accepted by a major American distribution company. I am leaving soon for Hollywood to discuss two possibilities for the lead role – James Coburn and George Peppard and I hope to direct it myself.

All of what has gone before reminds me of the guy who walked into a bar every night and, whilst holding his nose, ordered a large brandy.

This intrigued the bartender who asked him what he did for a living.

'I work with the circus.'

'Doing what?'

'I go into the ring after the elephants with a bucket and spade and clear up.'

'And what do they pay you for that?'

'Five pounds a night.'

'That's ridiculous. Come and work for me. I'll pay you ten.'

The brandy drinker stared hard at the bartender.

'I couldn't do that.'
'Why not?'
'You know what it's like... there's no people like show people.'

CURTAIN

TWO OTHER LIFE STORIES FROM QUADRANT BOOKS

— But Very Different —

Captain of the Queen
This is the autobiography of the most famous sea captain of them all. Captain Robert Harry Arnott is master of the *Queen Elizabeth*, the largest and most luxurious passenger liner afloat. Captain Bob, as he is affectionately known, first went to sea at the age of 17 with the Blue Funnel Line. CAPTAIN OF THE QUEEN tells the story of his full career, culminating in that glorious moment when he was appointed Captain of the most famous passenger liner ever built.

The most famous names in the world, from all walks of life, have sailed on the QE2.

Many of the stories told are taken from the Captain's personal log, and the text is augmented with many illustrations from his own private collection.

8⅜" × 5¼" (216 × 138 mm)
336 pages £6.95

Burma Siam Railway
Dr Robert Hardie spent three years as a prisoner of war and kept a secret diary conveying the hardships, monotony and humiliations which marked the course of the 'railway of death.'

The original of this Diary was buried in the cemetery at Chungkai for fear of discovery by the Japanese and dug up in 1945. Published for the first time 40 years after the completion of the railway, Dr Hardie's Diary tells the true story of the 16,000 Allied prisoners who died from sickness, exhaustion and malnutrition.

It is a remarkable contemporary record written by a cultivated objective and sensitive observer.

The text is illustrated with Robert Hardie's own wartime sketches and watercolours.

$9\tfrac{7}{8}''\times 6\tfrac{7}{8}''$ (252 × 175 mm)
196 pages   £6.95

Both books are available from all good bookshops

Quadrant Books Limited
Newcombe House, Notting Hill Gate
London W11 3LQ.   Telephone: 01-243 8501